This Book Belongs To

Book 15
Content and Artwork by
Gooseberry Patch Company

BRAVE INK PRESS

EDITORIAL STAFF
President and Editorial Director:
 Carol Field Dahlstrom
Art Director:
 Lyne Neymeyer
Photo Stylists: Carol Dahlstrom, Jennifer Peterson,
 Jan Temeyer
Craft Designers: Heidi Boyd, Sonja Carmon,
 Phyllis Dobbs, Katie LaPorte, Janet Petersma,
 Janet Pittman, Jan Temeyer
Director, Test Kitchen: Jennifer Peterson
Test Kitchen Professionals: Catherine Fitzpatrick,
 Barbara Hoover
Copy Editor: Elizabeth Burnley
Photography: Jay Wilde Photography;
 Primary Image, Dean Tanner
Video/Communications: Dr. Michael Dahlstrom

BUSINESS STAFF
Business Manager: Judy Bailey
Webmaster: Leigha Bitz
Production Manager: Dave Hollingsworth
Props/Studio Manager: Roger H. Dahlstrom
Locations: Sharon and Craig Northhouse,
 Jan Temeyer
Marketing/Social Media Manager:
 Marcia Schultz Dahlstrom

Hardcover ISSN: 2154-4263
Softcover ISSN: 2154-4263
Hardcover ISBN-10: 0-8487-3983-3
Hardcover ISBN-13: 978-0-8487-3983-6
Softcover ISBN-10: 0-8487-3984-1
Softcover ISBN-13: 978-0-8487-3984-3
10 9 8 7 6 5 4 3 2 1

OXMOOR HOUSE
Editorial Director: Leah McLaughlin
Creative Director: Felicity Keane
Brand Manager: Vanessa Tiongson
Senior Editor: Rebecca Brennan
Managing Editor: Rebecca Benton

Gooseberry Patch Christmas Book 15
Editor: Susan Ray
Art Director: Claire Cormany
Project Editor: Emily Chappell
Director, Test Kitchen: Elizabeth Tyler Austin
Recipe Editor: Alyson Moreland Haynes
Test Kitchen Professionals: Wendy Ball, R.D.; Victoria E. Cox;
 Stefanie Maloney; Margaret Monroe Dickey; Callie Nash;
 Karen Rankin; Catherine Crowell Steele; Leah Van Deren
Photography Director: Jim Bathie
Senior Photographer: Helen Dujardin
Senior Photo Stylist: Kay E. Clarke
Associate Photo Stylist: Katherine Eckert Coyne
Assistant Photo Stylist: Mary Louise Menendez

CONTRIBUTOR
Editor: Ashley Strickland Freeman

TIME HOME ENTERTAINMENT INC.
Publisher: Jim Childs
VP, Strategy & Business Development: Steven Sandonato
Executive Director, Marketing Services: Carol Pittard
Executive Director, Retail & Special Sales: Tom Mifsud
Director, Bookazine Development & Marketing: Laura Adam
Publishing Director: Joy Butts
Associate Publishing Director: Megan Pearlman
Finance Director: Glenn Buonocore
Associate General Counsel: Helen Wan

WOODSON

Christmas

Book 15

Christmas

Gooseberry Patch

Wishing all our family & friends the happiest of holidays!

Our Story

Back in 1984, we were next-door neighbors raising our families in the little town of Delaware, Ohio. Two moms with small children, we were looking for a way to do what we loved and stay home with the kids too. We had always shared a love of home cooking and making memories with family & friends and so, after many a conversation over the backyard fence, Gooseberry Patch was born.

We put together our first catalog at our kitchen tables, enlisting the help of our loved ones wherever we could. From that very first mailing, we found an immediate connection with many of our customers and it wasn't long before we began receiving letters, photos and recipes from these new friends. In 1992, we put together our very first cookbook, compiled from hundreds of these recipes and, the rest, as they say, is history.

Hard to believe it's been over 25 years since those kitchen-table days! From that original little Gooseberry Patch family, we've grown to include an amazing group of creative folks who love cooking, decorating and creating as much as we do. Today, we're best known for our homestyle, family-friendly cookbooks, now recognized as national bestsellers.

One thing's for sure, we couldn't have done it without our friends all across the country. Each year, we're honored to turn thousands of your recipes into our collectible cookbooks. Our hope is that each book captures the stories and heart of all of you who have shared with us. Whether you've been with us since the beginning or are just discovering us, welcome to the Gooseberry Patch family!

We couldn't make our best-selling cookbooks without YOU!

Each of our books is filled with recipes from cooks just like you, gathered from kitchens all across the country.

Share your tried & true recipes with us on our website and you could be selected for an upcoming cookbook. If your recipe is included, you'll receive a FREE copy of the cookbook when it's published!

www.gooseberrypatch.com

We'd love to add YOU to our Circle of Friends!

Get free recipes, crafts, giveaways and so much more when you join our email club...join us online at all the spots below for even more goodies!

Homespun Holiday

Cuddle up for a cozy Christmas that is sure to create happy memories of family holidays. Felt gingerbread men decorate the fresh evergreen tree as they dance around a Christmas Rose Garland stitched from print fabric. Sweet gingerbread cookie houses decorated with piped frosting fill the tree with home-sweet-home love. Foam balls are wrapped with warm nubby yarn for simple striped trims. A trio of vintage-style stockings adorn the mantle anticipating Santa's arrival. Gingham aprons are pressed and ready for holiday baking, and red and green apples fill a Welcoming Apple Basket lined with a gingham and calico print. So gather the family together to share in the best homespun holiday ever!

Look in your fabric basket to choose some calico prints and tiny checks to make a Christmas Rose Garland. The pieces are folded and spiraled to create the oh-so-sweet blooms. Colorful accents are added by stitching a special button to the middle of each flower.

Christmas Rose Garland

A beautiful way to showcase your fabric stash! Gingham and calico strips are folded, stitched and spiraled into cheery blooms. Each bloom is framed by a pair of rustic linen backed leaves. Red vintage buttons make the flower centers twinkle.

Dimensions: As long as desired.

- $1/4$ yard or less of assorted red gingham and calico cotton fabric
- $1/4$ yard green gingham
- $1/4$ yard linen
- $1/2$" red buttons
- off-white sewing thread
- $1/2$" woven natural trim
- sewing machine
- sewing needles
- cutting mat, straight edge and rotary cutter
- scissors
- hot-glue gun and glue sticks

1. Begin by cutting the flower strips. Set out your cutting mat, use a rotary cutter and straight edge rule to cut the red gingham and calico fabrics into 3" w by 18" long strips. **Note:** The length of the garland depends on how many flowers you make. Each fabric strip makes a single flower.

2. Fold and stitch each flower strip. Placing right sides together fold the strip lengthwise, lining up the cut edges together. Pin the folded layers together; repeat the process with the remaining strips.

3. Run each folded strip through your sewing machine, making a single straight seam to join the cut edges together. Turn each strip right side out. Poke $1/2$" of fabric into the top and bottom of the strip, this will conceal the unfinished cut ends.

4. Hand-stitch, gather, and spiral the flower strips. Starting with a single flower strip, use sewing needle and thread to hand-stitch along the seamed edge of the strip.

(continued on page 11)

5. Once you reach the end of the strip, leave the needle and thread attached. Slide the fabric toward the knot end of the thread. While gathering, it will shrink to approximately 10" long. Spiral the gathered strip into a flower. The strip should make 2 rotations.

6. Stitch the spiraled fabric together and add a button center. Using the attached needle, make multiple stitches across the back of the spiraled flower to hold the fabric in place. Before knotting the thread, stitch a button to the right side of the flower center. Repeat the steps to transform the remaining flower strips into flowers.

7. To cut and stitch the leaves, use the pattern (page 147) as your guide to cut out gingham leaves. You'll need to place a leaf between each flower so cut accordingly. Pin the

(continued on page 118)

Christmas Rose Garland

Gingerbread Man Ornaments

Run, run as fast as you can…you can't catch me, I'm the gingerbread man! Soft felt cookies are frozen in playful action. For stability, each ornament is made with 3 layers of wool felt. Mini rickrack, buttons and glass beads take the place of laborious embroidery. So quick to stitch, you'll want to whip up a dozen to share with family & friends.

- tracing paper
- pencil
- 2 shades of brown wool felt such as National Nonwovens
- white mini rickrack
- red 2-hole mini buttons
- 6 mm black seed beads
- embroidery floss in brown, and off-white
- off-white sewing thread
- embroidery and sewing needles
- sharp sewing scissors

(continued on page 118)

Gingerbread Man Ornaments

Create Gingerbread Man Ornaments with wool felt and scraps of rickrack. Make Nubby Yarn Trims by wrapping two colors of yarn around a foam ball. Home-Sweet-Home Gingerbread Cookies are the sweetest kind of ornament. Stir up an entire village of these special, tasty trims.

Nubby Yarn Trims
Instructions are on page 118.

Home-Sweet-Home Gingerbread Cookies
Nubby Yarn Trims

Home-Sweet-Home
Gingerbread Cookies

Home-Sweet-Home Gingerbread Cookies

You can make these tasty cottages as elaborate or simple as you like. Look at your own house for some sweet inspiration.

2 c. shortening
2 c. sugar
2 c. molasses
2 T. cinnamon
2 t. ground cloves
2 t. baking soda
1 t. salt
9 to 10 c. all-purpose flour

To make dough, heat shortening, sugar and molasses in a 5-quart saucepan over low heat until sugar dissolves, stirring constantly. Remove from heat; stir in cinnamon, cloves, baking soda and salt. Gradually work in flour until a stiff dough forms; turn dough out onto a lightly floured surface and knead in as much remaining flour as possible while still maintaining a smooth

consistency. Divide dough into 4 sections; wrap each in plastic wrap and refrigerate until ready to use. Dough should chill for at least 2 hours before rolling out.

(continued on page 119)

13

Vintage Christmas
Stocking Trio

Hung by the chimney with care, this Vintage Christmas Stocking Trio says, "Merry Christmas" with sweet embellishments so thoughtfully stitched on each one. Bits of lace, shell buttons, tiny printed fabrics, mini rickrack and layered chiffon trims make these stockings treasured heirlooms.

Vintage Christmas Stocking Trio

No holiday is complete without stockings hung by the fire. These simple beauties share the same calico, gingham or linen fabrics as the Christmas Rose Garland. Each stocking is embellished with strips of coordinating fabrics, rickrack, flowers and shell buttons. A simple trick makes lining and finishing each stocking a snap.

Note: Yardages given are for one stocking.
- tracing paper
- pencil
- $1/2$ yard of stocking body fabric such as calico, gingham or linen
- $1/4$ yard of accent fabric such as calico, gingham or linen
- $1/2$ yard ivory lining fabric such as muslin or cotton
- 2 foot length of rickrack or chiffon trim
- shell buttons (optional)
- die-cut fabric flowers and pieces of lace (optional)
- iron
- straight pins
- sewing needles
- scissors

1. Enlarge and trace the patterns (pages 154, 155) onto tracing paper adding a $1/4$" seam allowance to all sides of the patterns. Cut 2 pieces for the stocking body from the calico, gingham or linen fabric. Cut 2 pieces for the lining from the ivory fabric.

2. Decide which 2 fabrics (calico, linen or gingham) will complement the main stocking fabric. Then cut

(continued on page 119)

Checked fabric and green calico combine to make Silent Night Bedding Trims so festive and bright. Christmas-red rickrack adds just the right finishing touch. Create your own Holly-Inspired Place Setting by layering green, cream and red plates on a checked place mat. Then tuck some fresh holly into a clear glass ornament to complete the look.

Silent Night Bedding Trims

Who wouldn't love tucking into special Christmas bedding to dream of sugar plums on Christmas Eve?

Note: Yardages given are for twin size bedding and one pillow case.
- purchased cream color pillow case
- purchased cream color sheet set
- 1½ yards green checked cotton fabric
- ½ yard coordinating green print fabric for flat flange
- ½ yard plain green print fabric for piping
- 5 yards red mini rickrack
- sewing machine
- matching sewing thread
- small red buttons (optional)

(continued on page 120)

Silent Night
Bedding Trims

Holly-Inspired
Place Setting

Holly-Inspired Place Setting

What could be more inviting than a tablescape all decked out for the holidays? There is no need to purchase new dishes...just combine some of the ones you have to create a lovely place setting for each guest. Stack different colored plates that showcase Christmas colors, and set the dishes on a red and white checked place mat. Light votive candles to add warmth to the table. For a simple table favor, cut fresh holly and slide it into a clear glass ornament for take-away gifts.

Bring back memories of Grandma in the kitchen with vintage-style aprons. The gingerbread-brown Gingham Rickrack Apron is embellished with white rickrack and small stitches. The Christmas-Red Cross-Stitch Apron features simple cross stitches on the checked grid. Showcase red and green apples in a Welcoming Apple Basket made from country prints.

Gingham Rickrack Apron

Gingham Rickrack Apron
Tiny rickrack is couched with embroidery floss to create a sweet pattern on this vintage-style apron.

- 1 yard of brown-and-white $1/4$" gingham fabric
- scissors
- matching sewing thread
- 5 yards of white mini rickrack
- 3 yards of white medium rickrack
- 6 skeins of brown embroidery floss
- embroidery needle
- embroidery hoop

1. From the gingham fabric cut the following pieces: Cut one 24" long x 36" w piece for the apron front. Cut two $4^1/2$"x 36" pieces for the apron ties. Cut one 4"x 24" piece for the apron waistband. Cut one 6" w x $7^1/2$" long piece for the pocket. Press all pieces.

2. Referring to the pattern grid (page 156), use 3 strands of floss to couch the rickrack to the apron front starting 8" from the unfinished bottom of the apron front piece. (For Couching Diagram, see page 141.) Set aside.

3. Referring to the pattern grid (page 156), use 3 strands of floss to couch the rickrack to the apron waistband, starting $3/4$" from the bottom of the waistband. Set aside.

4. Referring to the pattern grid (page 156), use 3 strands of

(continued on page 120)

Christmas-Red Cross-Stitch Apron

Easy to stitch, cross-stitches are the embellishment on this classic apron that brings back Christmas memories.

- 1 1/2 yards red-and-white 1/8" gingham fabric
- coordinating sewing thread
- scissors
- 5 skeins of red embroidery floss
- embroidery needle
- embroidery hoop

(continued on page 120)

**Christmas-Red
Cross-Stitch Apron**

Welcoming Apple Basket

Tiny prints of red and green combine to make a sweet scalloped basket liner to hold red and green apples. The basket shown is 12"x 8" but you can adjust the liner to fit your favorite basket.

- tracing paper
- pencil
- scissors
- purchased basket in desired color and desired size
- 1/2 yard red-and-green print fabric
- 1/2 yard green checked fabric
- matching sewing threads
- 1 yard 1/8" cording for piping (optional)
- 1/4 yard tiny red print check for piping (optional)

(continued on page 121)

**Welcoming
Apple Basket**

What could be merrier than gathering family & friends together for a woodland holiday? On your outdoor adventure, be sure to pick up some of nature's findings so you can create an Acorn Garland and Stars of Sticks. Add some milkweed pods and holly with these natural beauties to dress up an evergreen tree in the forest. Create a cozy cover for your holiday arrangement with birch bark or bits of twine. Woodsy mushrooms are the inspiration for ornaments made from felt and embellishments. So bundle up and surround yourself with nature's beauty this holiday season!

Over -the- River and Through -the- Woods

Woodland
Gatherings

Choose your favorite pail to collect Woodland Gatherings to display for the holidays. Stars of Sticks and an Acorn Garland combine with natural milkweed pods and freshly picked holly for a Dressed-Up Evergreen.

Woodland Gatherings

Choose a favorite enamel pail or basket to showcase nature's beauty. Simply line the bottom with small sprigs of evergreen and then add handmade trims and other findings from nature to fill the container.

Stars of Sticks

Let nature form the most beautiful shape of the season... the star. Choose the size and type of stick that you like and then wire them together to form the star shape.

- paper
- pencil
- 5 short sticks each about 5" long
- hot-glue gun and glue sticks
- 24-gauge copper wire
- wire cutters

1. On paper, draw a star shape the size you want the finished star to be. Or, refer to the patterns (page 144) for size ideas. Lay the sticks on the shape overlapping as needed.
2. Use hot glue to secure the sticks in place. Let dry. Wrap copper wire at the joints where the sticks cross. Add a looped wire for hanging.

Woodland Gatherings

Stars of Sticks

Dressed-Up Evergreen

Dressed-Up Evergreen

Decorate an outside tree or pot a small tree in a container. Then add natural decorations such as milkweed pods, bits of fresh holly, Stars of Sticks and an Acorn Garland. Surround the base of the tree with pinecones to complete the look.

Acorn Garland

Little acorns and pinecones combine to form a garland of beautiful texture and shape.

- acorns
- small pinecones
- 26-gauge wire
- $1/8$" drill bit
- crafts glue

1. Drill the acorns and pinecones through the center of each piece. **Note:** If the tops of the acorns come off while drilling, glue back together.
2. Thread wire through the holes until the desired length of garland is achieved. Loop ends of wire to secure at each end.

Bark & Twine Arrangement

Bark & Twine Arrangement

Pieces of bark and twine add texture and color to a purchased container.

- large plastic or ceramic container
- potting soil
- fresh greenery
- pinecones
- sticks
- artificial holiday pokes of desired color
- pieces of found bark
- twine

1. Fill the container with potting soil. Arrange the fresh greenery as desired. Add sticks, pinecones and holiday pokes as desired.

2. Place the arrangement on a flat surface. Vertically stand up the bark around the container and tie tightly with twine.

Birch Bark-Wrapped Poinsettias

Instructions are on page 121.

Birch Bark-Wrapped Poinsettias

Birch bark trees release their bark naturally in the winter. So gather this beautifully textured bark to make Birch Bark-Wrapped Poinsettias. Fallen bark is wrapped with twine to make a Bark & Twine Arrangement. Wrap gifts naturally with Nature-Topped Packages.

Nature-Topped Packages

Nature-Topped Packages

Brown paper packages tied up with ribbons are embellished with found objects from nature to create stunning gift wraps.

- packages to be wrapped
- brown kraft paper
- ribbon in brown and green
- hot-glue gun and glue sticks
- found nature objects such as acorns, small pinecones and sticks
- greenery

1. Wrap the package with the brown paper. Wrap the ribbon around the packages overlapping or entwining the ribbons. Secure with tape on the back.

2. Hot-glue nature findings where the ribbons cross, layering the items as desired.

Felt-Trimmed
Mushroom

Fringe-Trimmed
Mushroom

Silk-Trimmed
Mushroom

Felt Mushroom Ornaments

The speckled red tops and luminous stems of woodland mushrooms look magical on the mossy ground and even better hanging from the branches of your Christmas tree. These beauties are made with felt, satin, vintage buttons, fringe trims and embroidery floss.

- tracing paper
- pencil
- wool felt such as National Nonwovens in burgundy, brown, pink, tan, squash
- polyester satin in off-white, tan
- fringe: polyester, leather, braided
- $1/4$" to $3/4$" buttons
- embroidery floss in pink, rose, gold
- sewing thread in red and tan
- polyester fiberfill
- leather cording
- sewing machine
- embroidery and sewing needles
- straight pins

1. Referring to the patterns (page 148) cut out the pattern

(continued on page 122)

Tiny Tree in Tin

Tiny Tree in Tin

Even the tiniest of trees can be showcased in a special tin to say "Merry Christmas!"

- vintage tin container such as a tin picnic basket
- small jar to fit in tin
- pinecones
- small evergreen tree
- small red jingle bells
- red-and-white striped cotton twine
- ½" w plaid ribbon

1. Set the tree into the glass jar and fill with water. Set the tree in jar into the tin container. Surround the tree with pinecones.
2. Cut small pieces of ribbon and tie onto the tree. String the jingle bells on the cotton twine and tie on the tree.

Felt Mushroom Ornaments seem to sprout overnight on the forest floor. Create your own version of these woodland shapes using wool felt and your choice of trims. And what could be simpler than tucking a miniature evergreen into a vintage tin basket? This Tiny Tree in Tin sports red jingle bells tied on with twine.

rick-rack and ribbon!

can't miss CHRISTMAS GIFTS

You want to give the most perfect gift to those special people near and far. What could be better than a handmade gift? Try rolling rickrack to make Rickrack Posies or get out the scrapbook paper to create a Handmade Note Card Set. Braid some embroidery floss…then add beads and charms to make Braided Bookmarks for that avid reader on your list. Need a quick, last-minute gift? Get out the canning jars and fill them with little goodies for personalized gift containers. Have fun making presents for everyone on your Christmas list. They'll treasure these handmade gifts forever!

Rickrack Posie

Kaleidoscope Magnets

Glue little pieces of art to the back of flat marbles to create colorful and clear holders for displaying special papers.

- flat glass marbles
- vinegar
- scissors
- crafts glue
- art from page 156 or original art
- $1/2$" flat round magnets

1. Be sure the flat marbles are clean and dry. Wipe off the marble with vinegar and let dry.
2. Photocopy the art on page 156 and cut out. **Note:** You may have to adjust the size of the art to fit the marble. Cut out the desired design. If making your own design, cut out a circle to fit the marble size from white cardstock. Draw design on paper with markers or fine pen.
3. Use your finger to add a thin layer of glue to the flat side of the marble. Place the art, color side down, on the marble. Glue the magnet to the back of the marble. Let dry.

Kaleidoscope Magnets

Rickrack Posies

Roll some rickrack to make the cutest little posies ever!

For each flower:
- one package of medium rickrack in desired color
- matching sewing thread
- sewing machine
- scissors
- scrap of wool or silk for leaf (for pin and hair pretty)
- $1/4$" w green ribbon (for package trim)
- 3"x 3" piece of muslin
- crafts glue

(continued on page 122)

Rickrack Posie Pin

Rickrack Posie Hair Pretty

Handmade
Note Cards

Handmade Note Cards

Handmade
Note Card Holder

Make a set of Kaleidoscope Magnets to dress up the fridge for the entire year! Freshly made by you, Rickrack Posies become pins, package tie-ons and hair pretties. Create a Handmade Note Card Set crafted from scrapbook papers and holiday motifs. Make a clever holder to store them all.

Handmade Note Cards & Holder

Everyone loves to write on a beautiful set of note cards! So why not make a pretty set for someone you care about?

- patterned paper
- coordinating cardstock
- invitation-sized (A2) plastic card box
- invitation-sized (A2) envelopes
- wide ribbon
- twine or cording
- self-adhesive nail heads
- trimmer
- scoring blade
- scissors
- adhesive, including strong double-sided tape and foam dots
- small hole punch
- seasonal punches or dies

For the Cards

1. From cardstock, cut card bases measuring 5 ½" x 8 ½". Score and fold in half. Plan the card message, and print onto white cardstock; cut out. Adhere artwork to the front of each card.

(continued on page 123)

Inspired Braided Bookmark

Charmed Braided Bookmark

Braided Bookmarks

A few strands of embroidery floss, beads and charms combine to make colorful book marks that will be a favorite gift.

For one bookmark
- 3 skeins of floss in desired colors
- beads in assorted colors with holes large enough for floss
- desired charms
- crafts glue
- masking tape

1. Unwrap floss and open up skeins. Double the 6-strand pieces so there are 12 strands of each color. Make the strands about 14" long or desired length. Lay the strands side by side and tape to a flat surface leaving about 4" above the tape.

2. Braid the strands until the desired length is done, leaving at least 4" at the end. Slide beads and charms at each end, separating the strands as desired. Knot the ends or weave both ends of the braided piece back up through the last bead or charm. Add a dot of glue to secure the end of the floss. Let dry.

For the book lover on your holiday list, create Braided Bookmarks that will be used and loved. Add inspirational jewelry findings or silver charms with colorful beads. Small-print fabrics are pieced together to make a homespun Nine-Patch Pot Holder. Present it wrapped around vintage kitchen tools.

Nine-Patch Pot Holder

Nine-Patch Pot Holder

A simple nine-patch quilt block becomes a hard-working pot holder just in time for Christmas baking.

Dimensions: Pot Holder shown is made using a 9" block

- small print cotton fabrics in desired colors
- $1/4$ yard of coordinating fabric for backing and binding
- heat-resistant interfacing
- matching sewing thread
- scissors
- sewing machine
- iron
- button

1. Cut nine $3^1/2$" fabric squares from light and darker print fabrics. Press. Lay the pieces out in the desired order you like.
2. With right sides together and using $1/4$" seams, sew 3 squares together to form strips, alternating lights and darks. See Diagram 1, page 124. Lay the 3 sets of strips together alternating darks and lights. See Diagram 2, page 124. Sew the strips together, alternating lights and darks, creating the block. See Diagram 3, page 124.
3. With an iron, press the seams to one side on the wrong side to allow them to lie flat.
4. Cut a 9"x 9" piece of heat-resistant interfacing. Set aside.

(continued on page 124)

Hair Pretties Jar

Sewing Kit Jar

Traveler's Jar

Personalize gifts for everyone on your Christmas list with Gifts in a Jar. Fill canning jars with hair pretties, sewing notions, traveling items or other much-appreciated goodies. Warm up winter drinks with sweet Needle-Felted Drink Cozies that are sure to be used all winter long!

Gifts in a Jar

To make your personalized gift jars, choose large wide-mouth canning jars to hold the goodies. Be sure the jar is clean and dry. Then fill with desired items. Draw around the flat lid top onto a piece of scrapbook paper, map or other paper to cover lid. Cut out. Place the jar lid and then the paper on the jar. Screw the top ring on jar. Wrap a ribbon around the jar and tie a bow.

Needle-Felted Tea Cozy

Snowman Cozy
Christmas Tree Cozy

• scrap of white felt for snow
• scrap of green felt for tree
• one skein gold metallic embroidery floss
• embroidery needle
• needle-felting tool such as Clover needle-felting tool
• small button
• 3" piece of narrow elastic

For the Snowman Cozy
• 4"x10" piece of blue felt or dimension to fit around chosen class or mug
• scrap of white felt for snowman body
• castaway sweater scraps
• one skein black embroidery floss
• one skein silver embroidery floss
• embroidery needle
• needle-felting tool, such as Clover needle-felting tool
• small button
• 3" piece of narrow elastic

(continued on page 124)

Needle-Felted Drink Cozies

Warm up those winter drinks with sweet little needle-felting wraps. These are so much fun to make that you'll want to make some for gifts and a few to keep for your holiday guests to use.

For the Christmas Tree Cozy
• 4"x10" piece of cream felt or dimension to fit around chosen class or mug

Button, button, who's got the button? You sort them, collect them, sew with them and treasure them! This year, let these little gems help you craft for Christmas as well! Layer buttons on a paper background to make a Framed Button Tree. Make a trio of Friendly Owls using wool and buttons…perched in your holiday tree or on a mantel, their captivating button eyes will watch over your holiday festivities. Cards that twinkle and engage, Snowflake and Tree Button Cards are so stunning they'll be brought out to display year after year. So find the button box and start choosing your favorite little buttons for those very special holiday projects.

Framed Button Tree instructions are on page 125.

Red, green and white buttons are layered on a frosted wreath to make a Stacked Button Wreath. Bit of felt and a few embroidery stitches combine to make a Colorful Circle Garland. Who would ever guess to make Friendly Owls using scraps of wool and buttons for eyes? Perch these little birdies on a birch bark branch for Christmas.

Stacked Button Wreath

A simple fresh evergreen wreath is dressed up for the holidays with vintage buttons and a dusting of spray snow. Add a festive holiday bow to complete the sweet wreath.

- small fresh green wreath
- spray snow
- assorted buttons
- scissors
- hot-glue gun and glue sticks
- red-and-white checked ribbon
- new or vintage belt buckle
- 24-gauge wire

(continued on page 125)

Colorful Circle Garland
Instructions start on page 125.

Colorful Circle Garland

Friendly Owls

Whooo can resist these smart woolen owls? They're all dressed up in woolen hounds-tooth and trimmed with wool felt. Touches of embroidery punctuate their chest and tuft their ears.

- tracing paper
- pencil
- ivory and hounds-tooth wool fabric scraps
- wool felt such as Woolfelt™ in brown, maroon and pink
- 1" and ½" buttons
- embroidery floss in brown, ochre
- sewing thread in brown, off-white and black
- polyester stuffing
- circle templates such as Sizzix big kick or hand cut 1¾", 1½", 1¼" and 1" circles
- sewing machine
- sewing and embroidery needles
- scissors
- optional pinking sheers

1. Trace the patterns (page 149). Cut out the owl's body and head. Cut 2 body pieces out of wool for each

(continued on page 126)

Winter-White Button Bracelet and Earrings

Timeless beauty, this lovely bracelet showcases your vintage button collection while dressing up your wardrobe. Shimmering mother of pearl buttons are framed with antiqued brass wire.

- 7$\frac{1}{2}$" of link antique brass chain
- white, ivory and shell buttons – approximately one button per chain link
- 20 gauge vintage brass wire
- lobster clasp
- oval rings, antique brass
- ear wires, antique brass
- round nose pliers
- needle nose pliers
- flush cutters
- jump rings

For the Bracelet

1. Prepare the wires for the button dangles. Use the flush cutters to cut the wires into 3" lengths. You'll need a length to attach each button. Use needle nose pliers to fold each wire 1" from the end. The wire will look like a hairpin.

2. Thread a button onto the wire, and shape the short end into a loop. Working with one wire at a time, string the wire ends through the front of the button. Use your round nose pliers to shape the short wire end into a loop $\frac{1}{2}$" above the button.

3. Link and wrap the button dangles onto the chain. Hook a shaped loop through the first link in the chain. Hold the loop in your needle nose pliers while you grab the long wire end with your round nose pliers. Tightly wrap the long wire around the base of the loop making 2 to 3 rotations. Use flush cutters to trim both wire ends flush against the finished dangle. Continue linking and wrapping button dangles until the remaining links have dangles hanging from them. Distribute the different button size and shapes along the length of the chain.

Winter-White Button Bracelet

Winter-White Button Earrings

(continued on page 127)

Snowflake Card

Tree Button Card

Snowflake and Tree Button Cards

If you have a button stash, this project is a perfect match. Combine a few of your two-hole treasures with decorative papers and embroidery floss. A dab of glue and a few stitches are all you need to create simply beautiful button greetings.

- tracing paper
- pencil
- blank white note cards and envelopes
- decorative scrapbook papers
- glue stick
- embroidery floss – silver and off-white
- stamp and stamp pad
- paper trimmer
- sharp sewing needle
- scissors

1. Select 2 coordinating papers for each card, one for the tree or circle snowflakes, and the other for the background. Use a paper trimmer to cut the background into a rectangle that fits your note card allowing a $1/2$" border on 3 sides and a 1" border at the bottom.
2. Trace the tree pattern (page 145). Cut out the tree shape from printed scrapbook paper. Cut assorted circles for the snowflakes.

(continued on page 127)

Choose your favorite tiny button treasures to create a Winter-White Button Bracelet and Earrings. Embroidery floss and buttons combine with decorative scrapbook papers to create Snowflake and Tree Button Cards…the perfect handmade greeting.

41

Festive Family FUN

Gather the family together to make some happy Christmas memories by creating some holiday projects. Copy favorite family photos to make a Picture-Perfect Gift Wrap. Or recycle those colorful Christmas cards into a Christmas Card Box or a Garland of Greetings. Turn puzzle pieces into a Holiday Puzzle Wreath with a little spray paint and some red jingle bells. Grab the crayons or the watercolors and let the little ones make a Little Artist Centerpiece for your holiday table. Need a fun table favor that the entire family will enjoy? Roll some wrapping paper to make Paper Poppers and fill them with candies or tiny gifts. No matter what you decide to craft, it will be more fun because you make it together.

Picture-Perfect Gift Wrap
instructions are on page 128.

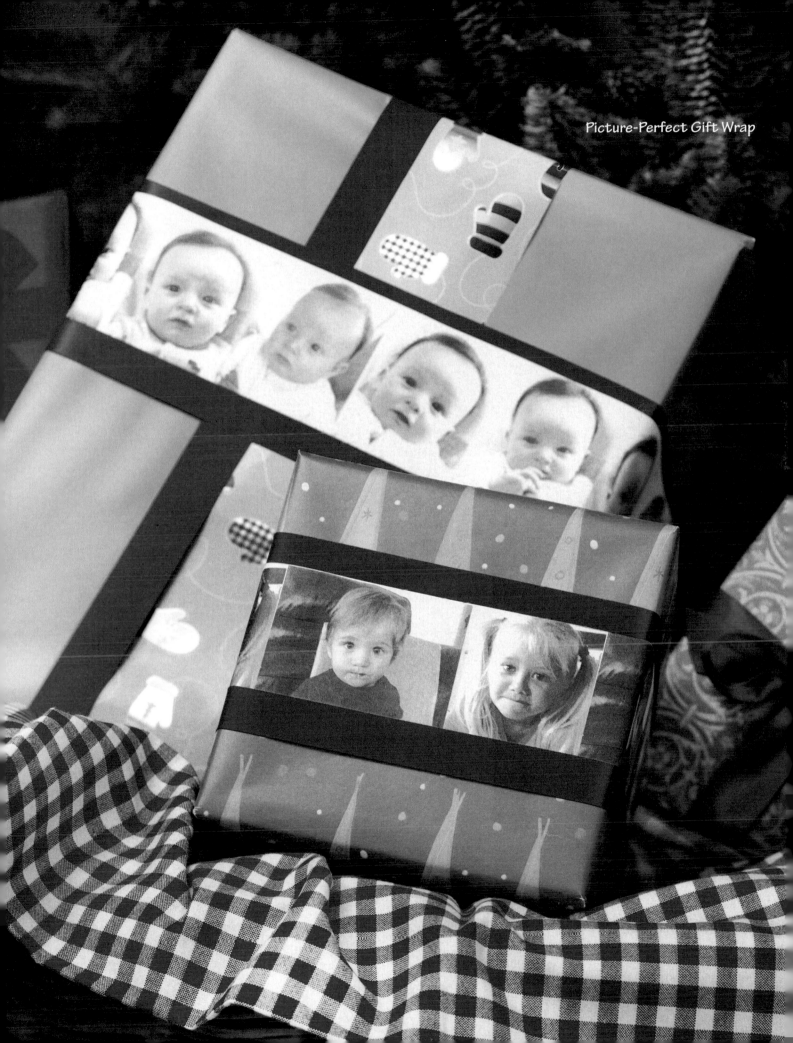

Picture-Perfect Gift Wrap

Christmas Card Box

Old Christmas cards shape up nicely to decorate a simple box to hold a tiny tannenbaum or other holiday goodies.

- old Christmas cards
- small cardboard box
- scissors
- crafts glue
- scrap of ribbon
- mini red rickrack

1. To cover the box, lay the box on the card fronts and draw around the card. Measure a card for each of the 4 sides of the box.
2. Glue the cards to each side of the box.
3. Glue the mini rickrack to the top edge, the bottom edge and the corners of the box.
4. Tie a bow with a scrap of ribbon and glue to the corner of the box.

Paper Poppers

Instructions are on page 128.

Christmas
Card Box

Paper
Poppers

Holiday Puzzle Wreath

Don't throw away those pretty Christmas cards! Recycle them to make a Christmas Card Box or a Garland of Greetings. A little green paint, some red jingle bells and old puzzle pieces are all it takes to make a Holiday Puzzle Wreath.

Holiday Puzzle Wreath

Put those mismatched pieces from cardboard puzzles to good use by making them into a wreath that everyone will enjoy.

• cardboard puzzle pieces
• old newspapers
• light green spray paint
• 9 red jingle bells
• crafts glue
• red-and-white checked ribbon

1. Place puzzle pieces on the newspaper and spray paint them with the green paint. Let dry. Turn over and spray the other side. Let dry.
2. Arrange the pieces in a circle. Layer other pieces on top of the first layer and glue in place. Add a third layer and glue in place. Let dry.
3. Glue the red jingle bells in sets of 3 on the wreath front. Tie a bow with the checked ribbon and glue to the top of the wreath.

Garland of Greetings
Instructions are on page 129.

Garland of Greetings

45

Paper Roll Picture Frame

Paper Roll Picture Frame

Recycle those brightly colored pages in magazines to decorate the edges of a picture frame. The kids can roll and glue them to the edges all by themselves!

- old magazines
- scissors
- crafts glue
- purchased picture frame with flat sides

1. Choose colorful pages from old magazines and cut strips about 2" to 3" w and 5" long. Roll the papers up from the short end and glue to secure. Make several of the rolled up pieces. Make different lengths if desired.

2. Glue the rolled pieces to the picture frame around the edges of the frame letting some pieces protrude out from the others. Make the pieces at bottom edges of the frame flush with the edge of the frame. Let dry.

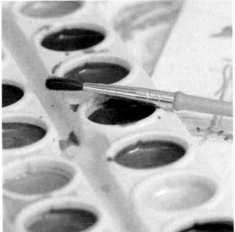

Get out a stack of old magazines and start rolling! Make a Paper Roll Picture Frame that becomes a family project and a perfect gift. Let those budding artists in the family show their artistic talents by making a Little Artist Centerpiece to share at holiday time.

Little Artist Centerpiece

Ask the little ones to draw or paint a picture for Christmas and then let the artwork become the center of attention at the holiday table.

- tall, straight-sided vase
- smaller, straight-sided vase to fit inside the large vase
- child's artwork
- scissors
- transparent tape
- water
- fresh flowers

1. Be sure the vases are clean and dry. Trim the artwork as necessary to fit inside the larger vase. Wrap the artwork around inside the vase and secure with the tape.
2. Put the smaller vase inside the larger one. Fill the smaller vase with water. Place flowers in the water.

Little Artist
Centerpiece

47

Peppermint Pretty

Make this Christmas oh-so-pretty by planning your holiday decorating around a peppermint candy theme. Fill a basket with sweet striped sticks to greet your guests. Roll up some pink and white felt to make a Felt Candy Wreath to hang on the front door. Use red and white cotton fabric to stitch a quick chair cover or a holiday apron. For a simple table favor, stack up ribbon candy to make a Ribbon Candy Tree. For a piece that is sure to become an heirloom, quilt a Peppermint Pinwheel Table Runner for your holiday table. Whatever striped project you choose, you can be sure that this holiday your decorating will be as sweet as can be!

Felt Candy Wreath

Felt Candy Wreath

Snatched right out of a magical land of candy, this peppermint wreath will add whimsy to your holiday décor. Soft strips of pink and white felt quickly roll up into beautiful candies. A simple dab of glue attaches them to a foam wreath form. This heirloom craft will inspire visions of sugar plums for years to come.

- foam wreath
- 100% wool felt such as National Nonwovens: 1 yard white, $\frac{1}{2}$ yard each of light pink and cotton-candy pink
- floral glue
- straight pins
- hot-glue gun and glue sticks
- rotary cutter, straight edge and cutting mat

(continued on page 129)

Rolled up strips of felt form the candy for a dreamy Felt Candy Wreath. Remember the old-fashioned ribbon candy that Grandma shared at Christmastime? Piled high, this favorite candy makes a festive little tree decoration for your holiday table.

Ribbon Candy Tree

Almost like magic, rows of peppermint striped ribbon candy stack up to create this very sweet tree.

- 1 box of peppermint-striped ribbon candy, such as Sevigny's Thin Peppermint Candy
- 1 round peppermint hard candy
- hot-glue gun and glue sticks

1. Carefully remove the candy from the box and plan the tree design by carefully breaking the candy to make 4 graduating sizes when stacked.
2. Hot-glue the candy together. Hot-glue the single peppermint on the top.

Note: Candy tree is for decoration only and not to be eaten.

Ribbon Candy Tree

Sweet Chair
Back Slip

Simply Stitched
Place Mat

Simply Stitched Place Mat

Add a little embellishment to a purchased place mat with a few simple stitches.

- purchased red place mat with holes as a decorative feature on the edges or plain red place mat
- embroidery needle
- pink embroidery floss
- scissors

1. Thread the needle with all 6 strands of the embroidery floss. If using a place mat with pre-made holes as a decoration, start at one corner and stitch back and forth through holes. Trim the ends.
2. If using a plain red place mat, use the running stitch to form a line around the edge of the mat. (See page 142 for Running Stitch Diagram.)

Striped & polka-dot fabrics are stitched together to make a Sweet Chair Back Slip...perfect for your kitchen chairs. Pink embroidery floss adds a little color to make a Simply Stitched Place Mat for your holiday table. Red & white fabrics and sweet candy combine to make a Peppermint Tablescape and a Candy Jar Table Favor.

Sweet Chair Back Slip

Don't forget to dress up your chairs with a little peppermint sweetness for the Christmas holiday!

For one chair cover:
- tracing paper
- pencil
- $1/2$ yard of red-and-white striped cotton fabric
- $1/3$ yard pink polka-dot fabric

(continued on page 130)

Peppermint Tablescape

Your table will sparkle with the sweetness of the season when you choose a color palette of red, white and pink. A simple red candle on a clear vintage holder surrounded by evergreen is all you need in the center of the table. Stack white plates on red place mats and then add a special table favor using a canning jar and peppermint candies. Wrap your chairs in fun printed fabrics and tuck a candy cane and greens in the pocket for a welcoming surprise for each guest.

Candy Jar Table Favor
Instructions are on page 130.

Peppermint Tablescape

This pretty Peppermint Pinwheel Table Runner is pieced using the classic pinwheel patchwork block as the focus of the piece. Happy colors and prints in pink, white and green make it a holiday favorite.

Peppermint Pinwheel Table Runner

Pieced to resemble a peppermint candy, this beautifully quilted table runner will grace your holiday table in style!

Note: All fabrics are 40" w. Use $1/4$" seam allowances throughout.

- 1 fat quarter or $1/4$ yard pink-and-white stripe fabric for pinwheels
- $1/2$ yard pink-and-white dotted fabric for pinwheel and binding
- $1/2$ yard white-on-white print fabric for background
- $1/3$ yard green-and-white print fabric for border
- 21" x 48" rectangle for backing
- 21" x 48" rectangle for batting

Cutting:

From pink-and-white stripe fabric cut:
Four $5^3/8$" squares. Cut each square in half diagonally.

From the pink-and-white dotted fabric cut:
Three $2^1/4$" w strips for binding.
Two $5^3/8$" squares. Cut each square in half diagonally.

(continued on page 130)

Peppermint Pinwheel
Table Runner

Peppermint Pinwheel Table Runner

Candy-Striped Cones

Pieces of striped scrapbook paper are rolled and trimmed with ribbon to make Candy-Striped Cones. You'll be in the holiday spirit when you wear your Candy Cane Apron to pass out the candy this year!

Candy-Striped Cones

Fill these paper cones with sugar candy and hang on your Christmas tree this year.

For one cone:

- tracing paper
- pencil
- One 12"x12" piece of striped or patterned medium-weight scrapbook paper
- 10" piece of $^3/_4$" w red-and-white striped ribbon
- 12" piece of $^1/_4$" w red-and-white polka-dot ribbon
- crafts glue
- snap clothespin
- awl
- peppermint candy to fill cones

(continued on page 132)

Candy Cane Apron

Candy Cane Apron

Red and white stripes combine with winter white rickrack to make a festive apron.

- tracing paper
- pencil
- 1 yard of red-and-white striped cotton fabric
- 3 yards of white rickrack
- scissors
- matching sewing thread

1. Trace patterns, and enlarge if necessary, (pages 150, 151) and cut out. Transfer patterns to the striped fabric. Cut out. Mark all dots on fabric using pencil. In addition, cut two 6"x 6" pieces of striped fabric for pockets.

2. With right sides together, stitch apron front seam together using a French seam. Press. Stitch waistband to top of apron front, pivoting at the center front.

3. Narrow hem edges and ends of ties. With right sides together, pin to sides of waistband, stitch. With right sides together, stitch waist band facing to waistband, starting at dot and across straight edge of waistband to other dot. Turn and press. Press under 1/2" at waistband facing raw edge and whipstitch closed.

4. Turn under 1/4" on pocket top edge twice and topstitch. Turn under 1/4" on sides and bottom of pockets and press. Position on apron front at marked dots. Topstitch in place. Place rickrack over stitched edges at sides and bottoms of pockets and topstitch in place.

5. Narrow hem sides and bottom of apron. Topstitch rickrack over the the hem.

in tHe nick of TIME

Christmas is almost here and you just can't wait! But can you get it all done? Sure you can! Make simple holiday displays using vintage clocks or bottles. Get out the paper punches to make Punched Luminarias. A rubber stamp and some fabric paint combine to make a Stamped Snowflake Towel that says "Merry Christmas" when you come into the kitchen. Whip up a pair of Quick Felt Stockings just in time for Santa. In minutes you can make Holiday Bolster Pillows using purchased kitchen towels and snippets of ribbon. So sit back and relax with a cup of hot chocolate…there is plenty of time to get ready for Christmas!

Clock Collection Holiday Display instructions are on page 132.

Clock Collection
Holiday Display

Dear Santa,
Please send me a doll
and a monkey
Love, Sarah

Wishes in a Bottle

Wishes in a Bottle

Vintage milk bottles line up with wishes for Santa Claus. Write special wishes for each person in the family on cream-colored paper. Then roll the wishes and tuck them into milk bottles or other clear containers. Rest Christmas ornaments on top of the bottles and arrange on the mantel or tabletop. Add some fresh greenery around the bottle to complete the festive look.

Quick Felt Stockings

Instructions start on page 132.

Quick Felt Green Stocking

Quick Felt White Stocking

Line Wishes in a Bottle on your holiday mantel. Let a purchased finished-edge fabric make the cuffs on Quick Felt Stockings. Light up the walkway with easy-to-make Punched Luminarias. Switch up your holiday decorating with Holiday Bolster Pillows made using purchased kitchen towels.

Punched Luminarias

Simple purchased gift bags cast a new light when they are punched and lighted. Set them on a table for shimmering holiday glow.

- purchased heavy-duty red gift bags
- scissors
- paper punches in desired shapes and sizes
- crafts knife (optional)
- votive candles in glass containers

(continued on page 133)

Holiday Bolster Pillows
Instructions are on page 133.

Punched Luminarias

Holiday Bolster Pillows

61

A Stamped Snowflake Towel is quick & easy to make using a purchased kitchen towel and a rubber stamp and fabric ink. Create your own beautiful serving or display dishes by making Stacked Vintage Dishes. Simply choose your favorite pieces and place them atop each other…then fill them with holiday goodies or vintage ornaments.

Stamped Snowflake Towel

Get every room of your holiday home ready for Christmas by making some special trims! For the kitchen, you'll love being greeted by this happy kitchen towel stamped with a favorite holiday motif.

- purchased cotton kitchen towel with smooth texture and open areas to stamp
- iron
- waxed paper
- snowflake stamp pad or other desired design
- fabric stamp pad ink
- piece of paper or paper plate

1. Choose a towel that has a flat surface and is not too nubby. A cotton towel works best. Wash and dry the towel before stamping. Press the towel.

2. Place the towel on a flat surface. Slide the waxed paper under the entire towel.

Stamped Snowflake Towel

3. Stamp the rubber stamp onto the fabric ink pad and then onto the piece of paper to test the paint. If satisfied with the results, stamp on the towel where desired. Let dry. Remove the waxed paper.

Stacked Candy Holder

Stacked Vintage Dishes

Don't have a cake stand or a pretty candy dish? Get out the vintage dishes and try stacking them atop each other for a fun and festive look this holiday season.

- vintage dishes such as tumblers, plates, sugar bowls or other dishes with flat surfaces
- floral tacky wax
- items to put on the dishes such as candy or ornaments

1. Set out the dishes that you plan to use, and experiment by balancing different combinations together. Try setting a small plate on top of an inverted sugar bowl. Or turn a goblet upside down and place a small salad plate on top. When you are satisfied with your choices, use a little floral tacky wax to secure in place. This can easily be removed later.

2. Fill flat areas with candy, ornaments or other items.

Vintage Ornament Display

63

wrapped-up goodies from the Kitchen

Favorite recipes made with love…what could be a better Christmas gift? And when they are presented in clever containers with handmade tags, they are extra special! Stir up a batch of Grandma's Brown Bread and tie with a paper band. Whip up some cupcakes and tuck them into decorated boxes. Bake Big Santa Cookies and slide one into a parchment envelope for a special treat. Dip some Holiday Pretzel Rods and arrange them in a paper covered box. All your gifts from the kitchen are sure to be cherished this holiday season!

Grandma's Brown Bread

Serve this hearty old-fashioned bread warm with homemade apple butter...it's the best!

1 c. molasses
2 c. buttermilk
2 eggs, beaten
¼ c. shortening, melted and
    cooled
2 c. all-purpose flour
4 c. whole-wheat, graham or bran
    flour
1 c. brown sugar, packed
2 t. baking soda
½ t. salt

Mix molasses, milk, eggs and shortening in a bowl; set aside. Combine remaining ingredients in a separate large bowl; add molasses mixture and stir until moistened. Pour batter into a greased 9"x5" loaf pan; let stand 20 minutes. Bake at 350 degrees for 45 minutes. Cool on a wire rack. Makes one loaf.

Kathleen Walker
Mountain Center, CA

Paper Band & Tag instructions are on page 134.

Grandma's Brown Bread
Paper Band & Tag

Everyone loves cupcakes! Why not give them as a sweet gift this year? Make cupcakes in the colors of Christmas…red and green! Red Velvet Christmas Cupcakes are a beautiful shade of red and taste oh-so-good. Decorate your own cupcake boxes using scrapbook papers, simple shapes and scraps of beautiful tulle.

Red Velvet Christmas Cupcakes
Red Velvet Christmas Cupcake Box

Red Velvet Christmas Cupcakes

This is a really old family recipe, so old my copy calls for a stick of "oleo." I use this family recipe throughout the year for several holidays. Of course it's a must at Christmastime. I hope everyone who tries these cupcakes makes it a family tradition also!

2 1/2 c. all-purpose flour
1 1/2 c. sugar
1 t. salt
1 t. baking cocoa
1 c. buttermilk
1 1/2 c. oil
2 eggs, beaten
1 t. vanilla extract
1-oz. bottle red food coloring
1 t. white vinegar
1 t. baking soda
cinnamon candies, white sprinkles

In a large bowl, sift together flour, sugar, salt and cocoa. Add buttermilk, oil, eggs and vanilla; mix well. Stir in food coloring. Mix vinegar and baking soda together in a cup. Add to batter; mix only until well blended. Pour batter into muffin tins lined with 24 cupcake liners. Bake at 325 degrees for 15 to 20 minutes, until a toothpick inserted in center tests clean. Cool slightly. Remove from muffin tins. Cool completely. Frost cupcakes with Cream Cheese Frosting. Decorate with cinnamon candies and white sprinkles. Makes 24 cupcakes.

Cream Cheese Frosting:

8-oz. pkg. cream cheese, softened
1/2 c. margarine
1 t. vanilla extract
6 c. powdered sugar

In a bowl, blend cream cheese, margarine and vanilla. Stir in powdered sugar until well mixed.

Peggy Frazier
Indianapolis, IN

(continued on page 68)

Christmas Cupcake Box instructions start on page 134.

So pretty and green for Christmas, Holiday Pistachio Cupcakes are easy to make! A box of candy is a sweet gift indeed. Fill it with Eggnog Fudge and Truffle Trios.

Holiday Pistachio Cupcakes

My mom has been making these great-tasting cupcakes for years.

18$\frac{1}{2}$-oz. pkg. yellow or
    white cake mix
$\frac{1}{2}$ c. milk
$\frac{1}{2}$ c. water
$\frac{1}{2}$ c. oil
5 eggs, beaten
2 3.4-oz. pkgs. instant pistachio
    pudding mix
green and white candies, green
    sugar

In a large bowl, blend together dry cake mix, milk, water, oil and eggs until smooth. Add dry pudding mix; stir well. Pour batter into muffin tins lined with 24 cupcake liners. Bake at 325 degrees for 15 to 20 minutes, until a toothpick inserted in center tests clean. Cool slightly. Remove from muffin tins; cool completely. Frost cupcakes with Cream Cheese Icing. Decorate with candies and sugar. Makes 24 cupcakes.

Cream Cheese Icing:

8-oz. pkg. cream cheese, softened
$\frac{1}{4}$ c. butter, softened
1 t. vanilla extract
16-oz. pkg. powdered sugar
3 to 4 T. milk
1 to 2 drops green food coloring

In a large bowl, blend cream cheese, butter, vanilla and powdered sugar. Add enough milk for a spreadable consistency; stir in food coloring.

Sharon Dennison
Floyds Knobs, IN

Holiday Pistachio Cupcakes
Pistachio Cupcake Box

Eggnog Fudge

Enjoy this wonderful nibbling at Christmastime!

2 c. sugar
1 c. eggnog
2 T. butter
2 T. light corn syrup
$\frac{1}{4}$ c. chopped pecans, toasted
$\frac{1}{4}$ c. slivered almonds, toasted
    and chopped
$\frac{1}{2}$ c. candied red cherries,
    chopped
1 t. vanilla extract

Combine sugar, eggnog, butter and corn syrup in a heavy 4-quart saucepan. Cook over medium heat, stirring constantly, until mixture comes to a boil. Wash down crystals from sides of pan using a pastry brush dipped in hot water. Insert a candy thermometer into mixture. Cook, stirring occasionally, until mixture reaches the soft-ball stage, 234 to 243 degrees on a candy thermometer. Remove from heat and cool, undisturbed, until temperature reaches 190 degrees, about 15 to 18 minutes. Stir in nuts, cherries and vanilla. Beat with a wooden spoon until fudge thickens and just begins to lose its gloss, about 5 to 8 minutes. Line a 8"x4" loaf pan with aluminum foil; coat with butter. Pour mixture into pan. Cool completely; remove from pan and cut into squares. Makes one dozen.

Gina McClenning
Nicholson, GA

Pistachio Cupcake Box instructions start on page 134.

Eggnog Fudge/
Truffle Trios
Candy Box

Truffle Trios

I teach Sunday school at church, and these cookie truffles were given to me at Christmastime. What a terrific treat!

16-oz. pkg. chocolate sandwich cookies
8-oz. pkg. cream cheese, softened
2   8-oz. pkgs. semi-sweet baking chocolate, melted
1 c. powdered sugar
2 c. nuts, finely chopped

Remove cookie cream centers to a bowl; set aside. Crush cookie wafers in a separate bowl; set aside. Add cream cheese to cream centers; blend well. Add cookie crumbs to cream center mixture; mix until blended. Roll cookie mixture into 42 balls, each about one-inch in diameter. Dip 14 balls into melted chocolate. Roll 14 balls into powdered sugar. Roll remaining balls in nuts. Place on parchment paper-lined baking sheets and refrigerate until firm, about one hour. Store truffles, covered, in refrigerator. Makes 3^1/$_2$ dozen.

Kristan Vaughn
Gooseberry Patch

Candy Box Instructions are on page 135.

Stir up a batch of Homemade Caramels and then present the sweet morsels in a folded brown paper container. A Big Santa Cookie is the best present for any Christmas cookie lover! Make them all Santas, or choose a shape for each person on your list.

Homemade Caramels

My grandma has made these caramels every Christmas for as long as I can remember. One year she hadn't gotten around to making caramels by Christmas Eve. Everyone complained so much that she went to the kitchen at 9 o'clock at night and whipped them up. That year we realized how important food traditions really are to our family... thanks, Grandma!

2 c. sugar
2 c. light corn syrup
2 c. butter
12-oz. can evaporated milk
1 t. vanilla extract

Place sugar and corn syrup in a heavy saucepan. Bring to a boil over medium-high heat; do not burn. Boil mixture, stirring constantly for about 15 to 20 minutes, until it reaches the thread stage, 230 to 233 degrees on a candy thermometer. Add butter. Once melted, add evaporated milk. Keep boiling an additional 15 to 20 minutes, until it reaches the firm-ball stage, 244 to 249 degrees on a candy thermometer. Remove from heat; add vanilla. Pour into a greased 15"x10" jelly-roll pan. When cool, cut into $1\frac{1}{2}$ to 2-inch squares. Wrap in small squares of wax paper. Makes about $1\frac{1}{2}$ dozen.

Andrea Heyart
Aubrey, TX

Homemade Caramels
Brown Paper Wrap

Brown Paper Wrap instructions start on page 135.

Big Santa Cookie
Parchment Cookie Sleeve

Big Santa Cookie

There is nothing better than a cut-out cookie at Christmastime!

1 c. butter, softened
1 c. sugar
1 t. vanilla extract
1 egg
2 t. baking powder
3 c. all-purpose flour

In a bowl, blend together butter and sugar. Blend in vanilla and egg. In a separate bowl, combine baking powder and flour; add one cup at a time to sugar mixture, blending well. Roll out on a lightly floured surface to $\frac{1}{8}$-inch thickness; cut into desired shapes. Bake on ungreased baking sheets at 400 degrees for 6 to 7 minutes; cool and frost with Creamy Frosting. Decorate as desired. Makes about 2 dozen.

Terry Ross
Converse, TX

Creamy Frosting:

Homestyle vanilla frosting…yummy on sugar cookies.

6 T. butter, softened
$1\frac{1}{2}$ c. powdered sugar
2 T. whipping cream
$\frac{3}{4}$ t. vanilla extract
Optional: food coloring

Combine butter, powdered sugar, cream and vanilla together in a medium mixing bowl; blend with an electric mixer on low speed until smooth. Divide frosting among 2 or 3 small bowls; tint to desired color. Use immediately. Makes one cup.

Becky Sykes
Delaware, OH

Parchment Cookie Sleeve Instructions are on page 136.

Gather the whole family together to make Holiday Pretzel Rods…what a sweet treat to give and to enjoy! Make a double batch of Gingerbread Creamer Mix so you'll have plenty for yourself while you wrap your holiday packages!

Holiday Pretzel Rods
Holiday Pretzel Container & Tag

Holiday Pretzel Rods

These little goodies are favorites every holiday season. Use colorful sprinkles for Christmas and blue and white for Hanukkah. A tall mug or glass measuring cup is perfect for melting the coating.

1 $1/2$ c. semi-sweet chocolate
    chips
$1/2$ c. creamy peanut butter
10-oz. pkg. large pretzel rods
chopped walnuts, chocolate or
    colored sprinkles

Microwave chocolate chips in a tall, narrow, microwave-safe container on high until melted, about 1 $1/2$ minutes. Add peanut butter and stir until combined. One at a time, dip pretzel rods two-thirds of the way into chocolate mixture; gently tap against side of container to remove excess. Immediately roll rod in desired garnish. Place on baking sheets lined with wax paper; let stand until completely set. Makes about 2 $1/2$ dozen.

Louise Beveridge
Phillipsburg, PA

Holiday Pretzel Container and Tag instructions start on page 136.

Gingerbread Creamer Mix
Creamer Mix Jar

Gingerbread Creamer Mix

This spicy mix is perfect for making a warm drink for those cold winter nights!

2 c. powdered non-dairy creamer
$1/2$ c. brown sugar, packed
1 t. cinnamon
$1/2$ t. allspice
$1/2$ t. ground cloves
$1/4$ t. ground ginger
$1/4$ t. nutmeg

Combine all ingredients in an airtight container; mix well. Seal tightly and attach instructions (below). Makes about $2^{3}/4$ cups.

Instructions:
Pour one heaping teaspoonful of mix in a mug of hot coffee or tea. Stir to dissolve. Makes one serving.

Creamer Mix Jar instructions are on page 137.

A jar of Hot Fudge Sauce is sure to be a sweet gift for anyone. Sugared Marble Cookies stack up to make a quick & easy cookie gift.

Hot Fudge Sauce

Ever since I was a little girl, at Christmastime my mom would make this hot fudge sauce and buy peppermint ice cream to go with it. It is absolutely to die for!

1 $\frac{1}{2}$ 1-oz. sqs. unsweetened baking chocolate
$\frac{1}{2}$ c. water
$\frac{2}{3}$ c. sweetened condensed milk
$\frac{1}{4}$ c. sugar
$\frac{1}{8}$ t. salt
peppermint ice cream, pudding or cake

Stirring constantly with a whisk, heat chocolate and water in the top of a double boiler over medium heat. Cook and stir until chocolate is melted, about 3 minutes. Add condensed milk, sugar and salt. Cook until thick and smooth. Serve over peppermint ice cream, pudding or cake. Serves 6.

Abby Kramer
Asheville, NC

Hot Fudge Sauce
Sweet Gift Jar

Hot Fudge
SAUCE

Sweet Gift Jar instructions are on page 137.

Sugared Marble Cookies
Striped Package Tag

Sugared Marble Cookies
A melt-in-your-mouth cookie!

1 c. shortening
1 c. sugar
1 $\frac{1}{4}$ t. vanilla extract
1 $\frac{1}{4}$ t. almond extract
1 egg
2 c. all-purpose flour
$\frac{1}{2}$ t. salt
$\frac{1}{2}$ t. baking soda
$\frac{1}{2}$ t. cream of tartar
1-oz. sq. baking chocolate, melted

In a bowl, blend shortening and sugar; add extracts and egg, blending until fluffy. In another bowl, sift together dry ingredients; add to shortening mixture. Drizzle chocolate over dough, a little at a time, and cut it in with a knife. Do not stir. Form dough into one-inch balls and place on ungreased baking sheets; flatten slightly with bottom of drinking glass dipped in sugar. Bake at 400 degrees for 8 to 10 minutes, until edges are golden. Makes about 3 dozen.

Liz Wilmot
Honeoye Falls, NY

Striped Package Tag instructions are on page 138.

Molasses Popcorn Balls

I remember going to my grandma's farm in the Catskill Mountains of upstate New York for Christmas. She would hang these popcorn balls from her Christmas tree in small plastic bags tied with curling ribbon. She would also have brown paper bags in every kitchen corner just full of them! Now I live in the same Catskill Mountains and carry on her tradition.

12 c. popped popcorn
1 T. butter, softened
$1/2$ t. salt
1 c. molasses
$1/2$ c. sugar

Place hot popcorn in a large bowl. Mix in butter and salt. In a small heavy saucepan over medium-low heat, bring molasses and sugar to a boil. Boil until mixture reaches the hard-crack stage, 290 to 310 degrees on a candy thermometer. Gradually pour molasses mixture over popcorn mixture; mix well. Shape into balls with well-buttered hands; cool on wax paper. Makes 9 to 10 balls.

Cindy Beach
Franklin, NY

Merry Christmas Wrap instructions start on page 138.

Molasses Popcorn Balls
Merry Christmas Wrap

Wrap individual Molasses Popcorn Balls in cellophane bags and tie with a jingle bell tag. Line a basket with gingham and fill it with Maple Nutty Scones for a special gift. Everyone loves Holiday Snack Mix. Present it in a pretty paper covered jar.

Maple Nutty Scones

1 egg, beaten
1/2 c. buttermilk
1 t. vanilla extract
2 T. maple syrup
1 t. maple flavoring
3 c. all-purpose flour
1/2 c. quick-cooking oats, uncooked
2 1/2 t. baking powder
1/2 t. baking soda
1/2 t. salt
1/2 c. sugar
3/4 c. butter
1/2 c. chopped walnuts
1/2 c. chopped pecans

Mix first 5 ingredients; set aside. In a separate mixing bowl, combine next 6 ingredients; cut in butter until mixture reaches cornmeal consistency. Stir in walnuts and pecans. Pour in egg mixture; stir with a fork to make a soft dough. Turn out onto a lightly floured board; knead to get a slightly uniform dough. Shape into a circle 1/2-inch to 3/4-inch thick; cut into 16 wedges. Place on a greased baking sheet; bake at 425 degrees for 16 to 18 minutes, until lightly golden. Makes 16.

Maple Nutty Scones
Basket Tag

Holiday Snack Mix

4 c. pretzel sticks
2 c. bite-size honey-flavored corn cereal
6 c. combination of bite-size crispy wheat, rice and
    corn cereal squares
3 c. bite-size sweetened graham cereal squares
3 c. mixed nuts
1 c. butter, melted
1/4 c. plus 2 T. brown sugar, packed
1/4 c. Worcestershire sauce

In a very large bowl, mix pretzels, cereals and nuts. Spread into 2 ungreased 15"x10" jelly-roll pans. In a small bowl, mix together remaining ingredients, stirring until brown sugar is dissolved. Pour over pretzel mix; toss to coat. Bake at 250 degrees for one hour, stirring every 15 minutes. Spread on wax paper to cool. Store in an airtight container. Makes about 18 cups.

Abigail Smith
Worthington, OH

Holiday Snack Mix
Snack Mix Jar

Basket Tag Instructions are on page 139.
Snack Mix Jar Instructions are on page 139.

Quick & Easy Holiday APPETIZERS

Start the celebration in style with quick & easy appetizers you'll love to make and share. Put on your best Christmas apron and present your guests with Cheese-Olive Hot Snacks and Feta Squares as you greet them at the door. Set out little cupcake liners filled with Christmas Crunch. Bake some Swedish Meatballs and serve on a holiday platter. And don't forget to make that yummy Dilly Bread Bowl that is sure to become a holiday tradition!

Christmas Crunch

Crunchy and sweet, this snack is a holiday favorite with our family!

$1/2$ c. butter
1 c. brown sugar, packed
$1/2$ c. chopped pecans
$2^1/2$ c. corn flake cereal

In a saucepan over medium-low heat, melt butter. Stir in sugar; bring to a boil, then immediately remove from heat. Add pecans and cereal; toss to coat. Spread on wax paper to cool. Break apart and store in an airtight container. Makes about 2 cups.

Kathleen Felton
Fairfax, IA

Christmas Crunch

Peanut Butter Popcorn

This recipe was handed down from a friend of the family. If you like, when you're done mixing, bake the popcorn on an ungreased baking sheet at 200 degrees for 20 minutes.

2 $3^1/2$-oz. pkgs. microwave
     popcorn, popped
$1/2$ c. margarine
$3/4$ c. brown sugar, packed
20 marshmallows
$1/4$ c. creamy peanut butter

Place popcorn in a large bowl; set aside. In a separate microwave-safe bowl, combine margarine, brown sugar and marshmallows. Microwave on high at one-minute intervals, stirring between each interval, until mixture is melted and smooth. Stir in peanut butter until well blended. Pour margarine mixture over popcorn; stir quickly to coat before it cools. Serves 8.

Amy Teets
O'Fallon, MO

79

Dilly Bread Bowl

They'll all be standing around the table enjoying the Dilly Bread Bowl filled with rich sour cream and mayonnaise. Serve with fresh cut veggies in bright holiday colors. Cheese-Olive Hot Snacks are a quick pick-up treat everyone is sure to like! They'll love the cheesy crust and the surprise olive in the middle.

Dilly Bread Bowl

If you are really in the Christmas spirit, decorate the top of this creamy dip with a sprig of fresh dill formed into the shape of a Christmas tree. Then cut out a carrot star for the top and use finely chopped red and yellow peppers for ornaments. How pretty!

1 round loaf pumpernickel bread
1 c. sour cream
1 c. mayonnaise
1 T. dill weed
1 1/2 t. seasoning salt
1 T. dried parsley
2 T. dried, minced onion
1 t. garlic powder
assorted cut-up vegetables
Garnish: dill weed

Hollow out the center of bread loaf; set aside. Cube removed bread; set aside. Combine remaining ingredients except vegetables and spoon into center of loaf. Cover and chill for 24 hours. Garnish if desired. Serve with reserved bread cubes and vegetables for dipping. Serves 8 to 10.

Charlene Blackburn
Overland Park, KS

Cheese-Olive Hot Snacks

My sister and I make these snacks as part of our Christmas Eve dinner celebration. Their cheesy goodness make them a popular appetizer anytime.

5-oz. jar sharp pasteurized
    process cheese spread
1/4 c. butter, softened
1/8 t. hot pepper sauce
1/8 t. Worcestershire sauce
2/3 to 3/4 c. all-purpose flour
5 3/4-oz. jar green olives with
    pimentos, drained
1/4 t. pepper

In a bowl, blend cheese and butter until fluffy; add sauces, mixing well. Stir in enough flour to reach a dough consistency. Wrap each olive with a small piece of dough; roll so the olive is completely covered. Place on ungreased baking sheets. Bake at 400 degrees for 10 to 12 minutes, until lightly golden. Makes 15 to 20 servings.

Bonnie Studler
Los Angeles, CA

Chutney-Topped Brie

I was a little worried about trying Brie because I thought there was some mystery to it. To my surprise, I found an easy recipe, and it turned out great! We enjoyed this over the holidays and will definitely add it to our list of family favorites.

8-oz. round Brie cheese
1/4 c. apricot or cranberry chutney
2 T. chopped almonds or walnuts
assorted crackers

Trim and discard rind from top of Brie round, leaving a 1/4-inch border. Place Brie in an ungreased ovenproof serving dish; top with chutney. Bake, uncovered, at 400 degrees for 10 minutes, or until it appears melted. Watch closely to ensure cheese doesn't seep out. Toast nuts in a small non-stick skillet over medium-low heat, stirring often, for 2 to 3 minutes. Sprinkle nuts over Brie. Serve warm with assorted crackers. Serves 8 to 10.

Kathy Harris
Valley Center, KS

Cheese-Olive Hot Snacks

Feta Squares

Pass around a tray of these snacks at your holiday party, or serve with a tossed salad for a special lunch.

8-oz. container crumbled
    feta cheese
8-oz. pkg. cream cheese, softened
2 T. olive oil
3 cloves garlic, finely chopped
1 loaf sliced party pumpernickel
    bread
1 pt. grape tomatoes, halved
2 to 3 T. fresh chives, finely
    chopped

In a bowl, mix cheeses, olive oil and garlic. Spread mixture on pumpernickel slices. Place on ungreased baking sheets. Top each square with a tomato half; sprinkle with chives. Bake at 350 degrees for 15 minutes. Serves 8 to 10.

Jane Kirsch
Weymouth, MA

Feta Squares

Nutty Cheese Ball

Enjoy this different twist to the cheese ball family!

8-oz. can crushed pineapple,
    drained
2 8-oz. pkgs. cream cheese,
    softened
1/3 c. raisins
1/2 c. chopped dates
1/2 c. chopped pecans
round buttery crackers

Mix together all ingredients except pecans and crackers; blend well. Shape into a ball. Roll in chopped pecans. Refrigerate until serving time. Serve with crackers. Serves 10.

Becca Jones
Jackson, TN

Nutty Cheese Ball

Swedish Meatballs

Little pieces of bread turn into Feta Squares that add a new flavor to your appetizer tray. Present a Nutty Cheese Ball on a pretty red dish. The gang will come back for more of your delicious Swedish Meatballs!

Swedish Meatballs

I always make a double batch of these meatballs! Plus, I triple the sauce recipe, so if any meatballs are left over, there will be enough sauce to reheat them in.

1 1/2 lbs. smoked ham, finely diced
1 lb. ground pork sausage
2 c. dry bread crumbs
2 eggs, beaten
1 c. milk
Garnish: chopped parsley

Mix together all ingredients and roll into 1 1/2 to 2-inch balls. Place on an ungreased 13"x9" baking pan or in a large roasting pan. Pour Sauce over meatballs and bake, uncovered, at 325 degrees for 1 1/2 hours, turning meatballs every 30 minutes. Garnish with chopped parsley. Makes about 2 1/2 dozen.

Sauce:
1/2 c. water
1/2 c. vinegar
1 1/2 c. brown sugar, packed
1 T. dry mustard

Mix together all ingredients in a small saucepan. Cook and stir over medium-low heat until smooth.

Jane Granger
Manteno, IL

Christmas Morning Favorites

See the smiles on Christmas morning when you wake them with goodies from the kitchen! Try a mix of favorite comfort foods and some recipes that have a little different twist. They'll love classics like banana bread, French toast and baked apples. But they'll also love your Spinach & Mozzarella Quiche and Ham & Gruyère Egg Cups that make the morning even more special. Everyone will surely be nibbling on Cinnamon Knots and Cranberry Christmas Canes while they open their presents. Merry Christmas everyone!

Dad's Famous French Toast

Dad's Famous French Toast

When I was growing up, my dad fixed French toast every Sunday morning from his own recipe. Oh, how we loved it then and still do!

4 eggs, beaten
$1/2$ c. milk
$1/3$ c. sugar
1 t. vanilla extract
$1/8$ t. cinnamon
1 loaf sliced white bread
Garnish: butter, pancake syrup

Mix eggs, milk, sugar, vanilla and cinnamon in a large bowl. Dip bread into mixture, one slice at a time. Spray an electric or regular griddle with non-stick vegetable spray. Add bread slices; cook over medium heat until golden on both sides. Serve with desired garnishes. Serves 8.

Annette Mullan
North Arlington, NJ

Mile-High Biscuits

These biscuits are light, fluffy and oh-so-good!

3 c. all-purpose flour
2 T. sugar
$4^1/2$ t. baking powder
$3/4$ t. cream of tartar
$3/4$ t. salt
$3/4$ c. shortening
1 egg, beaten
1 c. milk

In a large bowl, sift together dry ingredients. Cut in shortening with a pastry blender until mixture resembles coarse meal. Combine egg and milk in a separate bowl. Add to flour mixture all at once; stir with a fork just enough to make a soft dough that sticks together. Turn onto a lightly floured surface; knead gently 15 times. Roll to one-inch thickness. Cut with a floured 2-inch round biscuit cutter. Place biscuits one inch apart on an ungreased baking sheet. Bake at 450 degrees for 12 to 15 minutes, until golden. Makes 16 biscuits.

Sharon Dennison
Floyds Knobs, IN

85

Spinach & Mozzarella Quiche

Scottish Pancakes

My husband is Scottish and has fond memories of eating his mum's pancakes. It's only recently that I dared to try making them, for fear of utter failure when compared with mum's!

2/3 c. self-rising flour
1/2 T. baking powder
3 1/2 T. sugar
1 t. vanilla extract
1 egg
7/8 c. milk
1 to 2 T. butter
Garnish: Greek-style yogurt

Sift flour and baking powder into a bowl; add sugar and vanilla. Create a well; add egg to well and whisk together ingredients. Add milk gradually; mix until smooth. In a skillet over medium heat, melt butter. When butter starts to bubble, add 2/3 cup batter to skillet per pancake, forming 2-inch pancakes. When bubbles start to appear on surface of pancakes, flip; cook one to 2 minutes on each side. Serve topped with yogurt and Blueberry Syrup. Serves 2.

Blueberry Syrup:
1 c. blueberries
1/2 c. maple syrup

Place berries and syrup in a small saucepan over medium-low heat. Simmer for 2 to 3 minutes, until warmed through.

Chris Hutcheson
Sheffield, England

Spinach & Mozzarella Quiche

One of my friends from church insists on having a piece of this quiche whenever I make it…it's quick, easy and delicious!

5-oz. pkg. baby spinach
2 T. water
9-inch deep-dish pie crust
1 c. shredded mozzarella cheese
3 eggs, beaten
1/2 c. sour cream
1/2 c. half-and-half
nutmeg, salt and pepper
    to taste
Garnish: tomato

In a saucepan over medium heat, steam spinach in water for 2 minutes. Drain well; press moisture out of spinach and sprinkle spinach over pie crust. Sprinkle cheese evenly over spinach. Whisk together remaining ingredients and pour over cheese. Bake at 325 degrees for 50 minutes. Let cool for 10 minutes before cutting. Garnish with tomato. Makes 6 servings.

Patricia Smith
Tehachapi, CA

The aroma of Spinach & Mozzarella Quiche will bring them down the stairs on Christmas morning! Hearty Ham & Potato Casserole is so quick to fix and fills hungry tummies. Ham & Gruyère Egg Cups look so inviting when presented in individual Christmas-colored ramekins.

Ham & Potato Casserole

I first made this casserole when there was ham left over from Christmas. Now my family requests it each year...and every time we have leftover ham!

4 potatoes, peeled and cubed
1 lb. cooked ham, cubed
1/2 c. onion, chopped
10³/4-oz. can cream of mushroom
   or cream of chicken soup
1¼ c. milk
1½ c. favorite shredded cheese,
   divided
salt and pepper to taste

Ham & Potato Casserole

Place potatoes in a saucepan filled with boiling salted water; cook over medium-high heat until almost tender, about 12 to 15 minutes. Drain and place in a lightly greased 13"x9" baking pan. Sprinkle ham and onion on top of potatoes. Mix together soup, milk and one cup cheese; pour over top of potato mixture. Sprinkle with remaining cheese. Bake, uncovered, at 350 degrees for 25 minutes, or until hot and bubbly. At serving time, season with salt and pepper to taste. Serves 4.

Linda Ervin
Durant, OK

Ham & Gruyère Egg Cups

This recipe is always on our Sunday brunch table. It is easy, simple and tasty...very pretty too!

12 thin slices deli ham
³/4 c. shredded Gruyère cheese
1 doz. eggs
salt and pepper to taste
1 c. half-and-half
2 T. grated Parmesan cheese
Garnish: pepper

Spray a muffin tin or ramekin cup with non-stick vegetable spray. Line each muffin cup or ramekin with a slice of ham folded in half. Top each ham slice with one tablespoon Gruyère cheese, an egg cracked into the cup, a sprinkle of salt and pepper, one tablespoon half-and-half and 1/2 teaspoon Parmesan cheese. Place muffin tin or ramekins on a baking sheet. Bake at 450 degrees for 15 minutes, or until eggs are set. If using a muffin tin, allow baked eggs to cool for several minutes before removing them from the muffin tin. Cool slightly before serving in ramekins. Makes one dozen.

Sonya Labbe
Santa Monica, CA

Ham & Gruyère Egg Cups

Serve sweet Candied-Glazed Baked Apples for a special treat on Christmas morning. Bake plenty of yummy Cinnamon Knots to have on hand for the big day!

Candied-Glazed Baked Apples

These apples have a tasty zip to them!

3/4 c. sugar
1/3 c. red cinnamon candies
1 c. water
4 baking apples
2 t. lemon juice
1 T. butter, diced

Combine sugar, candies and water in a saucepan; bring to a boil, stirring until sugar dissolves. Reduce heat; simmer, uncovered, for 2 minutes. Remove from heat; set aside. Peel top third of each apple. Remove and discard core, leaving bottom intact. Brush top of apples with lemon juice; arrange in a lightly greased 8"x8" baking pan. Dot centers of apples with butter; brush generously with sugar-cinnamon glaze. Bake at 350 degrees, uncovered, for one hour; brush frequently with remaining sugar-cinnamon glaze. Serve warm. Serves 4.

Jackie Smulski
Lyons, IL

Holiday Fruit Bowl

My mom makes this year 'round, but it is especially refreshing in winter when fresh fruit isn't abundant. My children think it's a terrific way to eat fruit, because it tastes like dessert!

16-oz. pkg. frozen strawberries, partially thawed
15-oz. can mandarin oranges, drained
20-oz. can pineapple tidbits, drained and juice reserved
3.4-oz. pkg. instant French vanilla pudding mix
2 bananas, sliced

Combine strawberries, oranges and pineapple in a large bowl. In a small bowl, stir together dry pudding mix and reserved juice until smooth. Add to fruit mixture; gently stir to coat. Cover and refrigerate 2 to 3 hours. Stir to blend; fold in bananas. Serves 6.

Dallas Bieker
Manhattan, KS

Holiday Wassail

It's our family tradition to enjoy wassail while opening presents Christmas morning. The citrus-spice aroma fills the house and really puts us in the holiday mood!

3 qts. apple juice
2 1/4 c. pineapple juice
2 c. orange juice
1/2 c. sugar
3-inch cinnamon stick
1 t. whole cloves

Combine all ingredients in a saucepan. Simmer, covered, over medium-low heat for 30 minutes. Uncover; simmer for an additional 30 minutes. Strain; discard spices. Serves 10 to 12.

Tara Horton
Delaware, OH

Cinnamon Knots

My mom used to make these breakfast treats when I was small. I can remember helping to dip them and then tie the knots. They smell wonderful baking and taste even better!

1 env. active dry yeast
$^3/_4$ c. warm water, divided
$^1/_2$ c. shortening
1 c. plus 3 T. sugar, divided
$^1/_2$ c. milk
1 egg, beaten
$^1/_2$ t. salt
3 c. all-purpose flour
1 c. butter, melted
3 T. cinnamon

Dissolve yeast in $^1/_4$ cup very warm water, 110 to 115 degrees; set aside. In a saucepan over medium heat, combine remaining water, shortening and 3 tablespoons sugar. Stir until sugar dissolves. Remove from heat; add milk and cool slightly. Pour mixture into a large bowl; add egg, salt and yeast mixture. Add flour and mix well. Cover and let rise in a warm place until double in size, about one hour. Roll out dough on a floured surface to $^1/_2$-inch thick. Cut dough into 6-inch by $^1/_2$-inch strips. Place melted butter in a small bowl. Mix remaining sugar and cinnamon together in a separate bowl. Dip each strip into butter and then into sugar mixture. Tie each strip into a knot; place on greased baking sheets. Cover and let rise until double in size, about one hour. Bake at 350 degrees for about 12 minutes, until golden. Makes $2^1/_2$ to 3 dozen.

Connie Spivey
Blue Springs, MO

Cinnamon Knots

An all time favorite that everyone loves, Banana-Nut Bread will disappear from the goodie tray like magic! Try a new twist with your yeast bread this year by making Cranberry Christmas Canes. These little canes are filled with cranberries, raisins and pecans. What could be prettier on Christmas morning?

Banana-Nut Bread

This scrumptious recipe has been in my family for about 75 years. My grandmother lived in Bermuda and made this bread using bananas picked from the banana trees in her yard.

2 c. all-purpose flour
1 c. sugar
1 t. baking soda
$^{1}/_{4}$ t. salt
$^{1}/_{2}$ c. canola or safflower oil
2 eggs, beaten
3 very ripe bananas, mashed
1 c. chopped walnuts or pecans

Combine flour, sugar, baking soda and salt in a bowl; mix well and set aside. In a separate large bowl, mix oil and eggs; add bananas. Add flour mixture and mix well; stir in nuts. Pour batter into a greased 9"x5" loaf pan or two 7"x3" loaf pans. Bake at 350 degrees, 45 minutes for a regular loaf pan or 25 to 30 minutes for 2 smaller pans. Makes one regular loaf or 2 smaller loaves.

Carolyn Ayers
Kent, WA

Banana-Nut Bread

Cranberry Christmas Canes

Heat one cup milk just to boiling; cool slightly. Combine flour, sugar, salt and lemon zest in a large bowl. Cut in butter with a pastry blender until mixture resembles coarse meal. Dissolve yeast in warm water, 100 to 115 degrees. Add yeast mixture, milk and eggs to flour mixture; combine lightly. Refrigerate for 2 hours to 2 days. At baking time, prepare Cranberry Filling; divide dough into 2 parts. On a floured surface, roll out half of dough into an 18-inch by 15-inch rectangle. Spread half of Cranberry Filling over dough. Fold rectangle into thirds, bringing both short edges over top of the center; press to seal. Slice rectangle into 15 strips. Holding both ends, twist each strip lightly in opposite directions; pinch ends. Place on a greased baking sheet; bend over tops to look like candy canes. Repeat with remaining dough and filling. Bake at 400 degrees for 10 to 15 minutes. Cool on wire racks. Mix powdered sugar with vanilla and remaining milk; frost pastries. Makes 2$\frac{1}{2}$ dozen.

Cranberry Filling:
1$\frac{1}{2}$ c. cranberries, finely chopped
$\frac{1}{2}$ c. sugar
$\frac{1}{2}$ c. raisins
$\frac{1}{3}$ c. honey
$\frac{1}{3}$ c. chopped pecans
1$\frac{1}{2}$ t. orange zest

Cranberry Christmas Canes

My mother used this recipe for more than 40 years…she always made them for our Christmas breakfast. We really looked forward to munching on these sweet pastries while we opened our gifts!

1 c. plus 1 to 2 t. milk, divided
4 c. all-purpose flour
$\frac{1}{4}$ c. sugar
1 t. salt
1 t. lemon zest
1 c. butter
1 env. active dry yeast
$\frac{1}{4}$ c. warm water
2 eggs, beaten
$\frac{1}{2}$ c. powdered sugar
$\frac{1}{4}$ t. vanilla extract

Combine all ingredients in a saucepan. Bring to a boil over medium heat. Cook for 5 minutes, stirring frequently; remove from heat and cool.

*Laura Flores
Middletown, CT*

Delicious & Decadent Chocolate

Everyone loves chocolate! So be sure and make this sweet favorite a big part of your holiday entertaining. Whether you stir up Grandma's Chocolate Cake and dust it with powdered sugar, dress up Honey-Kissed Chocolate Cookies with red and green sprinkles, or present Rich Holiday Fudge in mini holiday cupcake liners, your family & friends will keep reaching for these oh-so-yummy chocolatey goodies!

Rich Holiday Fudge

Rich Holiday Fudge

This is a family recipe that my granny passed down to me. She received this recipe from a dear friend of hers in El Paso, Texas, when my Papa was serving in the war. It has never failed me and always turns out scrumptious.

4 1/2 c. sugar
1 1/2 c. margarine
12-oz. can evaporated milk
3 6-oz. pkgs. semi-sweet
    chocolate chips
1 t. vanilla extract
13-oz. jar marshmallow creme
2 c. chopped pecans or walnuts

In a large, heavy saucepan over medium-high heat, combine sugar, margarine and evaporated milk. Bring to a rolling boil; boil for 5 minutes, stirring constantly. Remove from heat; add remaining ingredients. Stir until smooth and chocolate is melted. Pour onto a greased 15"x10" jelly-roll pan. Let stand overnight, or until firm. Cut into one-inch squares. Makes 5 pounds.

Christy Bonner
Berry, AL

They'll be asking for a second piece of Chocolate Fudge Pie right after they open their presents! Rich, dense and full of chocolate flavor, Grandma's Chocolate Cake is a perfect cake to serve with peppermint ice cream.

Chocolate Fudge Pie

In memory of my mom Juanita Fears, I've created my own special traditions at Christmastime just as Mom did when I was little. This pie is one of them. The filling is so yummy, you can serve it without the crust!

5 T. baking cocoa
1 c. margarine, melted and cooled
    slightly
4 eggs, lightly beaten
$1/2$ c. all-purpose flour
2 c. sugar
1 t. vanilla extract
2 8-inch pie crusts
Garnish: whipped cream, sprinkles

In a large bowl, combine cocoa, margarine and eggs. Add flour and sugar; mix well. Stir in vanilla. Divide evenly into crusts. Bake at 375 degrees for 30 minutes. Makes 2 pies, 6 to 8 servings each.

Julie Marsh
Shelbyville, TN

Chocolate Fudge Pie

Chocolate Thumbprint Cookies

$1/2$ c. plus 1 t. butter, softened
    and divided
1 c. sugar, divided
1 egg yolk
2 T. plus 2 t. milk, divided
$2 1/4$ t. vanilla extract, divided
1 c. all-purpose flour
$1/3$ c. baking cocoa
$1/4$ t. salt
$1/2$ c. powdered sugar
24 milk chocolate drops

In a small mixing bowl, cream $1/2$ cup butter, $2/3$ cup sugar, egg yolk, 2 tablespoons milk and 2 teaspoons vanilla together until light and fluffy; set aside. Combine flour, cocoa and salt; add to butter mixture, beating until well blended. Refrigerate dough at least one hour; shape into one-inch balls. Roll in remaining sugar; place on lightly greased baking sheets. Press thumb gently into center of each ball; bake at 350 degrees for 10 to 12 minutes. While baking, blend together powdered sugar, remaining butter, milk and vanilla. When cookies are done baking, spoon $1/4$ teaspoon filling into each thumbprint; gently press chocolate drop on top of filling. Remove from baking sheets; cool completely on wire rack. Makes 2 dozen.

Ann Fehr
Trappe, PA

Grandma's Chocolate Cake

Make chocolate curls using a vegetable peeler and a chocolate bar; or make a chocolate frosting to top off this yummy cake.

3 c. all-purpose flour
2 c. sugar
1/3 c. baking cocoa
1/2 t. salt
2 t. baking soda
1 t. vanilla extract
3/4 c. oil
2 T. vinegar
2 c. cold water
Garnish: powdered sugar,
    chocolate curls

In a large bowl, mix together all ingredients in order given. Blend well; pour into a greased fluted round pan or 13"x9" baking pan. Bake at 350 degrees for 35 minutes, or until a toothpick tests clean. Cool: Dust with powdered sugar or frost with Chocolate Frosting. Top with chocolate curls if desired. Serves 12.

Chocolate Frosting:

1/3 c. butter-flavored shortening
1/3 c. baking cocoa
2 c. powdered sugar
1 1/2 t. vanilla extract
2 T. milk

Combine all ingredients; blend until smooth.

Regina Wood
Ava, MO

Grandma's Chocolate Cake

Cherry Brownie Cobbler

Chocolate and cherries together...yum! Bake a Cherry Brownie Cobbler in no time using a brownie mix and canned cherry pie filling. Honey-Kissed Chocolate Cookies will disappear from the cookie tray. Warm up on Christmas Eve with Sweet Chocolate-Almond Coffee.

Fudgy Pudding Cake

A super-easy way to turn a cake mix into something really special!

1 c. brown sugar, packed
$1/2$ c. baking cocoa
2 c. water
2 c. mini marshmallows
$18^1/2$-oz. pkg. chocolate
   cake mix
Optional: 1 c. pecan, peanut
   or walnut pieces
Garnish: whipped topping or
   vanilla ice cream

Mix brown sugar, cocoa, water and marshmallows in a greased 13"x9" baking pan; set aside. Prepare cake mix as directed on package; spoon batter over mixture in pan. Top with nuts, if desired. Bake at 350 degrees for 45 to 50 minutes, until a toothpick inserted in center tests clean. Serve warm or cooled, garnished as desired. Serves 16.

Wilda Bartenschlag
Lewisville, OH

Cherry Brownie Cobbler

I found this recipe while looking for something new to make for a Sunday dessert. Your family & friends will love this cobbler...it's delicious! The chocolate and cherries really complement each other.

20-oz. pkg. brownie mix
$1/2$ c. water
$1/2$ c. oil
1 egg, beaten
21-oz. can cherry pie filling
$1/4$ c. butter, softened
$8^1/2$-oz. pkg. yellow cake mix
Garnish: vanilla ice cream

Prepare brownie mix according to packaging directions, using water, oil and egg. Spread batter into a 13"x9" baking pan sprayed with non-stick vegetable spray. Bake at 350 degrees for 15 minutes; remove from oven. Spread pie filling over brownie layer; set aside. Cut butter into dry cake mix until crumbly. Sprinkle mixture over pie filling. Return to oven and continue to bake an additional 45 to 50 minutes, until filling is set. Cool completely; cut into squares. Serve topped with scoops of ice cream. Serves 10 to 12.

Amy Hunt
Traphill, NC

In a medium bowl, beat honey and butter until light and fluffy. Beat in flour, cocoa and baking soda. Place sprinkles in a separate bowl. With hands, shape dough into one-inch balls. Drop balls into sprinkles and roll gently to coat. Place balls on baking sheets that have been sprayed with non-stick vegetable spray. Gently press one chocolate drop into the center of each cookie. Bake at 350 degrees for 10 minutes. Remove to wire racks to cool. Makes 3 dozen.

Lisa Engwell
Bellevue, NE

Sweet Chocolate-Almond Coffee

Set out this warm, yummy drink for Santa on Christmas Eve and you'll have a happy St. Nick!

$1/4$ c. baking cocoa
$1/4$ c. instant coffee granules
$1/2$ c. sugar
$1/4$ c. plus 2 T. finely ground almonds, divided
$1/4$ t. salt
2 t. powdered non-dairy creamer
$4 1/2$ c. milk
Garnish: whipped cream

In an electric blender, combine cocoa, instant coffee, sugar, $1/4$ cup ground almonds, salt and creamer. Cover and blend on high speed for 10 seconds. Heat milk in a 2-quart saucepan. Do not boil. Add cocoa mixture to hot milk; stir to combine. Pour into mugs. Top each serving with a dollop of whipped cream and a sprinkling of the remaining 2 tablespoons of the ground almonds. Makes 5 to 6 servings.

Honey-Kissed
Chocolate Cookies

Sweet Chocolate-
Almond Coffee

Honey-Kissed Chocolate Cookies

My youngest daughter loves these cookies and begs to make them every year. Both my girls help roll the cookie dough in the sprinkles and then top them with a chocolate drop. And with no eggs in the batter, they can lick the bowl too!

1 c. honey
6 T. butter, softened
2 c. all-purpose flour
1 c. baking cocoa
$1/2$ t. baking soda
red and green sprinkles
3 doz. milk chocolate drops, unwrapped

Slow-Cooker goodness

What could be cozier than to have your holiday fare cooking in the slow cooker as you wrap your packages for Christmas? Time is precious this season, so let the slow cooker help you make everything perfect. Plan a soup supper the night before Christmas and let the Christmas Eve Chili simmer while you go to church. Start the Sweet & Saucy Spareribs early in the day as you prepare for a holiday party. Cranberry Pork Chops can be the main dish on Christmas day and Slow Cooked Mac & Cheese is sure to be the kid's favorite! So grab the slow cookers and let them do the work as you sit back, relax and enjoy some extra stress-free time this holiday season!

Christmas Eve Chili

Christmas Eve Chili

A good bowl of chili is appreciated year 'round, but especially in chilly weather! Serve with a cast-iron skillet of cornbread or crisp corn chips…yum!

2 lbs. ground beef
1 green pepper, chopped
1 onion, chopped
16-oz. can kidney beans
15^1/$_2$-oz. can diced tomatoes
10-oz. can chili-style diced
    tomatoes with green chiles
8-oz. can tomato sauce
1-oz. pkg. chili seasoning

In a large skillet, brown beef, pepper and onion together; drain. Mix beef mixture with remaining ingredients in a slow cooker. Cover and cook on low setting for 2 to 4 hours, until hot and well blended. Makes 6 to 8 servings.

Madge Shepard
Franklin, NC

Country Corn Pudding

With four kinds of corn, this new twist on an old favorite is sure to be scrumptious!

16-oz. pkg. frozen corn
2 11-oz. cans sweet corn & diced
    peppers
14^3/$_4$-oz. can creamed corn
6^1/$_2$-oz. pkg. corn muffin mix
^{3}/$_4$ c. water
^{1}/$_4$ c. butter, melted
1 t. salt

Mix all ingredients well; pour into a slow cooker. Cover and cook on low setting for 5 to 6 hours, stirring after 3 hours. Makes 8 servings.

Angela Lively
Baxter, TN

Chicken Cordon Bleu

The Swiss cheese in this Chicken Cordon Bleu melts perfectly in the slow cooker. Got a hungry gang at Christmastime? Feed your hungry family with Homestyle Chicken Stew...they'll ask for more!

Chicken Cordon Bleu

I always used to fix this dish in the oven when we lived up north. When we moved to Florida, I was really glad to find a slow-cooker version so I didn't have to heat up the kitchen!

4 to 6 boneless, skinless chicken breasts
4 to 6 slices deli ham
4 to 6 slices Swiss cheese
$10^3/_4$-oz. can cream of mushroom soup
$^1/_4$ c. milk
cooked egg noodles
Garnish: paprika

Place each chicken breast between 2 pieces of wax paper; flatten with a meat mallet. Remove wax paper. Top with a slice of ham and a slice of cheese. Roll up and secure with wooden toothpicks. Arrange chicken rolls in a slow cooker, making 2 layers if necessary. Blend soup and milk; pour over chicken. Cover and cook on low setting for 4 hours, or until chicken juices run clear. Serve chicken rolls over noodles. Top with sauce from slow cooker; sprinkle with paprika. Serves 4 to 6.

Beth Kramer
Port Saint Lucie, FL

Homestyle Chicken Stew

This is so good on a chilly autumn or winter day, along with homemade bread...mmm! If you don't have any celery on hand, just add 1/2 teaspoon celery seed from the spice rack.

1 lb. boneless, skinless chicken
    breasts, cubed
2 c. potatoes, peeled and cubed
1 stalk celery, sliced
2 carrots, peeled and sliced
14 1/2 oz. can chicken broth
6-oz. can tomato paste
1/2 t. paprika
1/4 t. pepper
1/4 t. dried thyme
1 1/2 T. cold water
1 T. cornstarch

In a slow cooker, combine all ingredients except water and cornstarch. Mix together well. Cover and cook on low setting for 7 to 8 hours, or on high setting for 3 1/2 hours. About 30 minutes before serving time, stir water and cornstarch together and stir into stew. Cook, covered, for an additional 30 minutes, or until thickened. Serves 4.

Jennifer Oglesby
Brownsville, IN

Savory Spuds

Potluck-perfect and oh-so-easy! Depending on what's in the cupboard, sometimes you can use cream of chicken, mushroom or cheese soup. They're all tasty!

2 lbs. new potatoes, peeled
10 3/4-oz. can cream of
    celery soup
1/4 c. sour cream
2 T. water
2 T. green onions, chopped
2 cloves garlic, minced
1 t. dill weed
1/2 t. salt

Place potatoes in a lightly greased slow cooker. Mix together remaining ingredients and add to potatoes; stir well. Cover and cook on low setting for 5 to 6 hours. Makes 4 to 6 servings.

Slow-Cooker Sage Stuffing

I use this recipe every Christmas because it's so delicious...it frees up space in the oven too.

14 c. bread cubes
3 c. celery, chopped
1 1/2 c. onion, chopped
1 1/2 t. to 1 T. dried sage
1 t. salt
1/2 t. pepper
1 1/4 c. butter, melted

In a very large bowl, combine all ingredients except butter; mix well. Add butter and toss. Spoon into a lightly greased slow cooker. Cover and cook on low setting 4 to 5 hours. Makes 8 to 10 servings.

Brenna Carey
Shickshinny, PA

Homestyle Chicken Stew

Slow-Cooked Mac & Cheese

This tastes just like the old-fashioned macaroni & cheese that Grandma used to make. It is delicious quick to make!

8-oz. pkg. elbow macaroni, cooked
2 eggs, beaten
12-oz. can evaporated milk
1 1/2 c. milk
3 c. shredded sharp Cheddar
   cheese
1/2 c. margarine, melted
1 t. salt
pepper to taste
Optional: grape tomatoes,
quartered

Mix all ingredients together and pour into a lightly greased slow cooker. Cover and cook on low setting for 3 to 4 hours. Sprinkle servings with tomatoes, if desired. Makes 6 to 8 servings.

Mary Alice Veal
Mars Hill, NC

Slow-Cooked Mac & Cheese

Sweet & Saucy Spareribs

These scrumptious ribs are just plain yummy any time of year!

2 lbs. pork spareribs, sliced into
   serving-size portions
$10^3/4$-oz. can tomato soup
1 onion, chopped
3 cloves garlic, minced
1 T. brown sugar, packed
1 T. Worcestershire sauce
2 T. soy sauce
1/4 c. cold water
1 t. cornstarch

Place ribs in a stockpot and add water to cover. Bring to a boil; reduce heat and simmer for 15 minutes. Drain; arrange ribs in a slow cooker. Mix together remaining ingredients except cold water and cornstarch; pour over ribs. Cover and cook on low setting for 6 to 8 hours. When ribs are tender, place them on a serving platter; cover to keep warm. Pour sauce from slow cooker into a saucepan over medium-high heat. Stir together cold water and cornstarch; stir into sauce and bring to a boil. Cook and stir until sauce has reached desired thickness. Serve ribs with sauce. Makes 4 servings.

Susie Backus
Gooseberry Patch

Sweet & Saucy Spareribs

Cranberry Pork Chops

Slow-Cooked Cooked Mac & Cheese is real comfort food they'll love this holiday season. Serve Sweet & Saucy Spareribs and Cranberry Pork Chops at your holiday meal. Having these tasty entrées in slow cookers will leave oven space for baking the last-minute rolls and desserts.

Cranberry Pork Chops

One of our favorite meals! So easy to prepare, but it looks and tastes likes you put a lot of time into it. I first tried it during the holiday season, and my family loved it so much that I now serve it several times a year.

6 pork chops
$^1/_2$ t. salt
pepper to taste
16-oz. can jellied cranberry sauce
$^1/_2$ c. cranberry juice cocktail
    or apple juice
$^1/_4$ c. sugar
2 T. spicy mustard
$^1/_4$ c. cold water
2 T. cornstarch

Season pork chops with salt and pepper; place in a slow cooker. Combine cranberry sauce, juice, sugar and mustard in a bowl; pour over pork chops. Cover and cook for 6 to 8 hours on high setting. Shortly before serving time, remove pork chops to a platter; keep warm. Combine cold water and cornstarch in a saucepan. Cook over medium heat, stirring continuously, until mixture becomes thick. Add liquid from slow cooker to saucepan and boil until thickened. Serve pork chops with sauce. Makes 6 servings.

*Jill Ball
Highland, UT*

Slow-Cooker Baked Apples

Delectable as either a side or a dessert! Sometimes I'll even fill the slow cooker late at night so we can enjoy them for breakfast.

8 Jonathan or Granny Smith
    apples, cored
$^1/_3$ c. raisins
$^1/_3$ c. chopped nuts
$^1/_3$ c. brown sugar, packed
1$^1/_2$ t. apple pie spice
2 T. margarine, sliced
$^1/_2$ c. apple cider
1 T. lemon juice

Remove peel from top $^1/_3$ of apples. Mix raisins, nuts and brown sugar; spoon into apples. Arrange apples in a greased slow cooker. Sprinkle with spice; dot with margarine. Mix cider and lemon juice and drizzle over apples. Cover and cook on low setting for 8 hours. Serves 8.

*Eva Jo Hoyle
Mexico, MO*

Christmas Caroler GOODIES

Greet holiday carolers at the door with sweet and savory treats they are sure to find noteworthy. Wish them a Merry Christmas by offering a plate of holiday cookies. Start with Sweet Music Cut-Out Cookies…a crispy sugar cookie decorated with piped frosting notes. Then share colorful Italian Cookies and Old Fashioned Molasses Cookies with a cup of warm Sycamore Farm Christmas Drink. For a special tiding of good joy, serve Jalapeño Puffers and Cheesy Party Squares to warm their voices. The carolers will be singing your praises when they taste the yummy treats you have in store for them!

**Sweet Music
Cut-Out Cookies**

Sweet Music Cut-Out Cookies

These cookies were frosted with a pastel colored icing and piped with musical staff and notes...perfect for Christmas Carolers!

3 c. all-purpose flour
1 t. baking powder
$^1\!/_2$ t. cinnamon
$^1\!/_4$ t. nutmeg
1 c. butter, softened
1 $^1\!/_4$ c. sugar
1 egg, beaten
1 t. vanilla extract
Garnish: icing

Stir together flour, baking powder, cinnamon and nutmeg. In a separate bowl, blend butter with sugar until light and fluffy. Beat in egg and vanilla. Beat in flour mixture until well combined. Cover dough and chill 3 hours. Divide dough in half; roll out on a well-floured surface. Cut with cookie cutters. Place 2 inches apart on greased baking sheets. Bake at 375 degrees for 8 to 10 minutes, until lightly golden. Cool and frost with Royal Icing (page 119). Decorate as desired. Makes 2 to 3 dozen.

*Kimberly Freeman
Mountain Grove, MO*

Old Fashioned Molasses Cookies will stack up well for cookie lovers this holiday season! A rich, dense drop cookie, Italian Cookies are a colorful addition to your holiday cookie plate.

Old Fashioned Molasses Cookies

This is my great-grandmother's recipe… handed down through our family, it's always a favorite.

³/₄ c. shortening
1 ¹/₂ c. sugar, divided
1 egg
4 T. molasses
2 c. all-purpose flour
2 t. baking soda
1 t. cinnamon
¹/₂ t. ground cloves
1 t. ground ginger

Blend together shortening, one cup sugar, egg and molasses until fluffy; set aside. Combine flour, baking soda, cinnamon, cloves and ginger together; gradually mix into molasses mixture. Cover and chill dough for 30 minutes. Shape dough into walnut-size balls; roll in remaining sugar. Place on ungreased baking sheets about 2 inches apart; bake at 350 degrees for 10 minutes. Cool on baking sheet one minute; remove to cooling rack. Makes about 4 dozen.

Amie Forgeron-Wheeler
Torrance, CA

Old Fashioned Molasses Cookies

Italian Cookies

These light, sweet cookies disappear quickly at family gatherings and get-togethers!

6 c. all-purpose flour
2 T. baking powder
¹/₂ t. salt
3 eggs
1 ¹/₂ c. sugar
²/₃ c. milk
1 T. vanilla extract
¹/₂ lb. shortening, melted
    and cooled
Garnish: frosting, sugars

Combine flour, baking powder and salt in a large mixing bowl; set aside. Blend eggs, sugar, milk and vanilla together; mix in cooled shortening. Stir into flour mixture; drop by tablespoonfuls onto ungreased baking sheets. Bake at 450 degrees for 8 to 10 minutes, until golden brown. Cool; frost and sprinkle with colored sugars. Makes about 6 dozen.

Frosting:

4 c. powdered sugar
¹/₄ c. milk
¹/₂ c. butter, softened
2 t. vanilla extract

Combine all ingredients in a large mixing bowl; blend on low speed for one minute. Increase speed to medium; blend until fluffy, about 2 minutes.

Suzanne Morell
Valley Springs, CA

Italian Cookies

Grandma's Peanut Sponge Candy

Everyone looked forward to receiving my grandmother's peanut candy as part of their Christmas gift. People still ask me for her recipe, even after thirty years!

3 c. sugar
1 c. light corn syrup
$^{1}/_{2}$ c. water
1 $^{1}/_{2}$ c. raw peanuts
$^{1}/_{2}$ c. butter, softened
3 T. baking soda
$^{1}/_{2}$ t. salt

Mix sugar, corn syrup and water in a heavy saucepan over medium heat. Continue to cook, stirring constantly, until mixture reaches the hard-ball stage, or 250 to 269 degrees on a candy thermometer. Add peanuts and cook until it reaches the hard-crack stage, or 290 to 310 degrees. Remove from heat. Stir in butter, baking soda and salt. Pour into an ungreased 15"x10" jelly-roll pan. Cool and break into pieces. Makes 2 dozen servings.

Janet Haynes
Bowling Green, KY

For a super-sweet treat, stir up a batch of Grandma's Peanut Sponge Candy to share this holiday season. Need a warm drink for a cozy winter night? Mix up Sycamore Farm Christmas Drink and serve to your guests...it will warm their hearts and tummies!

Grandma's Peanut Sponge Candy

Sycamore Farm
Christmas Drink

Oatmeal Crinkles

Have a plate of these yummy cookies ready for the carolers as they come to your door. They'll sing a happy tune!

1¼ c. sugar, divided
1 t. cinnamon
1 c. shortening
1 c. brown sugar, packed
2 eggs
1 t. vanilla extract
1 t. almond extract
2 c. all-purpose flour
1 t. baking powder
1 t. baking soda
1 t. salt
2½ c. long-cooking oats,
    uncooked
1½ c. raisins

Combine ¼ cup sugar and cinnamon together; set aside. Cream shortening, remaining sugar, brown sugar, eggs and extracts together in a large mixing bowl; set aside. In another mixing bowl, combine remaining ingredients; stir well. Add to sugar mixture; mix well. Roll into walnut-size balls; roll in sugar and cinnamon mixture. Place 2 inches apart on ungreased baking sheets; bake at 350 degrees for 10 minutes. Cool on baking sheet for 2 minutes; remove to cool on wire rack. Makes about 5 dozen.

*Krista Stames
Beaufort, SC*

Sycamore Farm Christmas Drink

The holidays are near when I begin making this drink at our family home in the country, appropriately named Sycamore Farm.

64-oz. bottle cranberry juice
64-oz. bottle apple juice
½ c. orange juice
1 T. cinnamon
1 T. whole cloves

⅔ c. sugar
Garnish: orange slices,
    cranberries

Combine all ingredients except garnish in a large stockpot over medium heat. Stir often until heated through. Remove cloves. Garnish with orange slices. Makes 16 cups.

*Penny Arnold
Louisville, IL*

Warm and yummy, Cheesy Party Squares are quick to make and pop in the oven right before serving. Frozen puff pastry makes Jalapeño Puffers a cinch to make. The pepper and cheese combination will be a holiday hit!

Cheesy Party Squares

An easy recipe we have loved for many years. These can be made ahead and frozen before baking…just thaw and pop in the oven when you're ready!

1 lb. ground beef
1 lb. ground Italian pork
    sausage
1 t. dried oregano
$\frac{1}{2}$ t. garlic powder
salt and pepper to taste
1 t. Worcestershire sauce
16-oz. pkg. pasteurized
    process cheese spread,
    cubed
1 loaf sliced party rye bread
Garnish: green pepper strips

In a skillet over medium heat, brown beef and sausage; drain. Stir in seasonings and Worcestershire sauce. Add cheese spread; mix and heat until completely melted. Spread onto party rye slices. Place on lightly greased baking sheets. Bake at 350 degrees for 10 minutes, or until hot and bubbly. Top with a green pepper strip. Serves 8 to 10.

Eleanor Dionne
Beverly, MA

Cheesy Party Squares

Jalapeño Puffers

Jalapeño Puffers

I ran out of ingredients to make batter once and found a long-lost package of puff pastry in the freezer. I figured, why not try this instead? It's fast and less messy than regular batter...plus you don't need a fryer!

9 to 12 jalapeño peppers
8-oz. pkg. cream cheese
8-oz. pkg. sharp Cheddar cheese
17.3-oz. pkg. frozen puff pastry,
    thawed

Cut jalapeños in half lengthwise; remove stems, seeds and ribs. Cut cheeses into strips to fit inside jalapeños. In each jalapeño, layer a strip of cream cheese, then a layer of Cheddar. Cut the puff pastry dough into 9 to 12 squares; stretch to fit around jalapeños. Wrap a dough square around each jalapeño; overlap seams and pinch closed. Place on ungreased baking sheets. Bake at 400 degrees for 15 to 20 minutes, until golden. Let cool on wire racks for a few minutes before serving. Makes 9 to 12.

Pia Cummins
Captain Cook, Hawaii

Perfectly Potluck

What fun to see all the yummy delights that arrive at a holiday potluck! Hot dishes, breads, cookies and desserts…they all are welcome at these fun family & friends get-togethers. Pack up Chicken & Dressing Bake and Grandma's Best Crescent Rolls to share…they'll disappear quickly at the church Christmas program. Roll out Christmas Cookie Favorites for your most cherished friends at the holiday potluck party. Almost out of time? Stir up an Easy Cherry Cheesecake in just a few minutes. So grab your table service and enjoy a happy holiday potluck together!

Chicken & Dressing Bake

Chicken & Dressing Bake

A great dish for family, company or church gatherings.

2 6-oz. pkgs. cornbread
   stuffing mix
1 t. dried sage
$^1/_4$ t. pepper
1 onion, finely chopped
4 stalks celery, finely chopped
2 $10^3/_4$-oz. cans cream of
   chicken soup
2 c. chicken broth
2 c. shredded Cheddar cheese,
   divided
4 boneless, skinless chicken
   breasts, cooked and cut in
   half lengthwise

In a large bowl, mix together stuffing mix, sage and pepper. Add onion and celery. Add soup, broth and one cup cheese to stuffing mixture; mix well. Place stuffing mixture into a 13"x9" baking pan that has been sprayed with non-stick vegetable spray. Place chicken on top of stuffing mixture. Top with remaining cheese. Bake, covered, at 350 degrees for 30 minutes. Makes 8 servings.

Dueley Lucas
Somerset, KY

Easy Beef Pot Pie

My kids love when I put the pie crust in muffin tins and serve individual pot pies!

1 lb. lean ground beef, browned
   and drained
$10^3/_4$-oz. can cream of potato
   soup
$10^3/_4$-oz. can cream of mushroom
   soup
$^1/_2$ c. beef broth
2 c. frozen mixed vegetables
1 t. garlic powder
salt and pepper to taste
2 9-inch pie crusts

Mix together all ingredients except pie crusts. Line an ungreased 9" pie plate with one pie crust. Pour beef mixture into crust; top with second crust. Seal edges; cut a slit in top of crust. Bake at 425 degrees for 30 to 35 minutes, until golden. Makes 6 servings.

Sarah Stillman
Salt Lake City, UT

Turkey Meatloaf
with Cranberry Glaze

Try a new twist using turkey by baking a Turkey Meatloaf with Cranberry Glaze to share at your holiday event. Everyone will be reaching for Grandma's Best Crescent Rolls. This easy yeast bread recipe can also be made into other roll shapes.

Potluck Meatballs

Spoon these yummy meatballs into crusty hard rolls or serve over pasta. Pass the Parmesan cheese, please!

1 1/2 lbs. ground beef
1 1/4 c. Italian-seasoned dry bread
　　crumbs
1/4 c. fresh parsley, chopped
2 cloves garlic, minced
1 onion, chopped
1 egg, beaten
28-oz. jar spaghetti sauce
16-oz. can crushed tomatoes
14 1/4-oz. can tomato purée

In a large bowl, combine all ingredients except spaghetti sauce, tomatoes and tomato purée. Mix by hand and form into 16 meatballs; set aside. In a slow cooker, stir together remaining ingredients. Add meatballs to sauce mixture and turn to coat. Cover and cook on low setting for 6 to 8 hours. Makes 4 servings.

Connie Bryant
Topeka, KS

Turkey Meatloaf
with Cranberry Glaze

I like to change things up each year for Christmas dinner. I made this recipe last year and discovered it's such a yummy alternative to traditional holiday fare!

16-oz. can jellied cranberry
　　sauce, divided
1/2 c. chili sauce or catsup
1 1/4 lbs. lean ground turkey
1/2 lb. ground pork
1 egg, beaten
1 c. soft bread crumbs
1 onion, finely chopped
3/4 t. poultry seasoning
1/2 t. salt
1/8 t. pepper

Mix together 1/3 cup cranberry sauce and chili sauce or catsup. In a bowl, combine turkey and remaining ingredients. Add 1/3 of cranberry sauce mixture. Mix until well blended. Spoon into an 8"x4" loaf pan that has been sprayed lightly with non-stick vegetable spray. Bake, uncovered, at 350 degrees for one hour. Top with remaining cranberry sauce mixture and bake an additional 10 minutes. Let stand for 10 minutes before slicing. Serve with remaining cranberry sauce. Serves 6.

Penny Sherman
Cumming, GA

Grandma's Best Crescent Rolls

Grandma's Best Crescent Rolls

My grandmother's rolls have always been a favorite at our family and church dinners. Grandma used a pie cutter to cut the dough into wedges. These make excellent cinnamon rolls too!

1/4 c. water
1 env. active dry yeast
1/4 c. sugar
3/4 c. warm milk
1/4 c. oil
3/4 t. salt
3 c. all-purpose flour
1/4 c. butter, melted

Heat water until very warm, about 110 to 115 degrees. In a large bowl, dissolve yeast in warm water. Stir in sugar, milk, oil and salt. Add enough flour to make a stiff dough; knead until smooth and elastic. Place dough in a separate greased bowl; turn to coat. Cover and let rise until double in bulk. Punch down dough; divide in half.

On a floured surface, roll out each half into a 12-inch circle. Spread melted butter on dough; cut each circle into 12 wedges. Starting at the large end of each wedge, roll up and place in a greased 13"x9" baking pan. Cover and let rise a second time. Bake at 350 degrees for about 20 minutes, until golden. Makes 2 dozen.

Marsha Overholser
Ash Grove, MO

Easy Cherry Cheesecake

My mom and I make this simple no-bake dessert every year for Christmas. Enjoy!

8-oz. pkg. cream cheese, softened
1 c. sugar
1/2 c. cold milk
1 env. whipped topping mix
1/2 t. vanilla extract
2 9-inch graham cracker crusts
21-oz. can cherry pie filling

Blend together cream cheese and sugar with an electric mixer on medium speed until smooth, about 2 to 3 minutes. In a separate bowl, combine cold milk, whipped topping mix and vanilla. Beat with an electric mixer on high speed for 4 minutes. Lightly fold milk mixture into cream cheese mixture. Pour mixture into crusts; cover and refrigerate overnight. Drizzle with cherry pie filling right before serving. Makes 2 cheesecakes, 6 servings each.

Angela Rowe
Ontario, Canada

Easy Cherry Cheesecake

Raisin Spice Bread

This is my grandmother's recipe…it's over 100 years old! This scrumptious bread is very moist, yet it has no eggs in it.

1 c. shortening
3 c. water
3 c. sugar
16-oz. pkg. raisins
1 t. ground ginger
1 t. ground cloves
1 t. nutmeg
1 t. cinnamon
1/8 t. salt
5 c. all-purpose flour
2 t. baking soda
Optional: chopped nuts to taste

Raisin Spice Bread

In a large saucepan over medium heat, combine shortening, water, sugar, raisins, spices and salt. Bring to a boil; boil for 5 minutes, stirring occasionally. Remove from heat; cool completely. Add remaining ingredients; mix well. Pour batter into 2 greased and floured 9"x5" loaf pans. Bake at 350 degrees for one hour, or until center tests done. Makes 2 loaves.

Nancy Neff Bell
Shawnee Mission, KS

Christmas Cookie Favorites

This is my great-grandmother's recipe. For as long as I can remember, these were made only at Christmas to share with family & friends. Frost with a favorite frosting and then pipe designs on the shapes that your family loves.

1 c. butter, softened
2 c. sugar
3 eggs, beaten
1 t. anise extract
1 1/2 t. baking soda
2 T. milk
5 c. all-purpose flour
1 1/2 t. cream of tartar
Garnish: frosting, colored sugars

Beat butter thoroughly. Add sugar, a little at a time, and blend thoroughly. Add eggs and extract. Dissolve baking soda in milk; add to butter mixture. Sift flour with cream of tartar. Add flour mixture to butter mixture; mix well. Turn out onto a floured board. Roll to 1/2-inch thick. Cut into desired shapes. Place on lightly greased baking sheets. Bake at 450 degrees for 7 minutes. Frost and decorate as desired. Makes 4 dozen.

Stacey Peterson
Huntingburg, IN

Frosting:
4 1/2 c. powdered sugar
6 T. butter, melted
6 T. milk
2 t. vanilla extract

Combine all ingredients in a large mixing bowl; blend on low speed for one minute. Increase speed to medium; blend until smooth, about 2 minutes.

Tina Knotts
Cable, OH

Christmas Cookie Favorites

Stir up an Easy Cherry Cheesecake in the nick of time for the holiday potluck. A dense and delicious quick bread, Raisin Spice Bread slices beautifully to take along to any dinner event. What could be better than Christmas Cookie Favorites? Make them in your favorite holiday shapes and watch them disappear.

Project Instructions

3 layers together to stabilize them. Separate 3 strands of embroidery floss and thread them through the embroidery needle. Join the 3 layers together by whipstitching around the outside edge. Begin and end at the top of the head.

5. Once you've encircled the man, use the remaining length of floss to form a hanging loop. Knot the floss 3" above the top of the head, trim away the excess.

Christmas Rose Garland

continued from page 11
(also shown on pages 9–11)
gingham leaves onto the linen, spacing them 3/4" apart. Machine stitch the gingham leaves to the linen, encircling the inside edge of the green leaves and creating a center vein down the middle. Once all the leaves are stitched, begin cutting them out. Leave a 1/4" linen border around each leaf. (The fraying of the fabric is part of the charm and rustic design.)

8. Alternate the different patterned flowers down the length of the trim, spacing them 3" apart. Hot-glue or stitch them to the trim. Once the flowers are in position on the length of garland, place a leaf between each of the flowers.

Gingerbread Man Ornaments

continued from page 12
(also shown on pages 9, 12)

1. Trace patterns (pages 146–147) and cut out. Sandwich the darker brown felt between 2 layers of lighter brown felt. Carefully pin the pattern to 3 layers of felt. Using sharp fabric scissors, cut through all layers at once. This will ensure that they are exactly the same size.

2. Embellish the top body layer, starting with the rickrack trim. Cut 4 lengths of rickrack, one for each of the wrists and ankles, and another length for the waist. Add 1/2" to each length so that the rickrack can tuck under the outside edge. Use sewing needle and white thread to hand-sew each piece of rickrack to the body. Start and end the seam by catching the end of the folded-under rickrack in your stitches.

3. Add the eye, mouth and buttons. Continue using sewing needle and white thread to stitch the bead eyes to the top of the head and 2 red buttons down the gingerbread man's body front. Switch to a full strand of floss and embroidery needle to make 3 small stitches for his mouth.

4. Stack the finished top body over the other two body layers. Pin the

Nubby Yarn Trims

(also shown on page 13)
Gather the whole family together to make these fun, striped trims.

For one ball

- 3" foam ball such as Styrofoam
- 2 yards red nubby yarn
- 2 yards gold nubby yarn
- straight pins
- crafts glue
- scissors

1. Place yarn colors side by side and work with the 2 fibers as if they are one fiber.

2. Starting at the top of the ball, make a loop with the yarns and pin in place. Wind the yarns around and around the ball keeping the yarns side by side. Add a drop of glue under the yarns as you work to keep in place. Use pins to temporarily keep the yarn in place.

3. To finish, glue ends in place, trim yarn and secure with pin.

Home-Sweet-Home Gingerbread Cookies

continued from page 13
(also shown on pages 9–13)

1. Enlarge and trace pattern pieces (page 143) and cut out. Trace onto parchment paper, and cover with clear plastic laminate. Set aside.

2. Roll about ¼ of the dough out on a large sheet of parchment paper, sprinkling with additional flour to keep dough from sticking to rolling pin. Roll to about ¼" thickness.

3. Place pattern pieces on top of dough, leaving at least ½" between them. Cut around the pieces with a sharp knife. Use a drinking straw to make a hole in the top of each cookie for hanging.

4. Place parchment with dough cutouts on a large flat baking sheet. Bake at 375 degrees for 8 to 10 minutes, until cutouts are firm in center. Remove from oven.

5. Carefully place the pattern pieces back on top of the cutouts and re-trim with a sharp knife. Open hole if

necessary. Remove pattern pieces from cookie top and return cutouts to oven for 2 to 4 more minutes, until edges are lightly browned and gingerbread is dry. Remove parchment with cutouts to a rack or counter to cool.

6. Referring to photos, page 13, pipe white icing on houses. Let dry. Add ribbon for hanging.

Royal Icing:
3 T. meringue powder
⅓ c. plus 2 T. warm water
4 ½ c. powdered sugar
½ t. cream of tartar

In a medium bowl, combine all ingredients. Beat with an electric mixer on low speed until combined. Beat on high speed for 7 minutes, or until very thick and stiff. Keep covered with plastic wrap when not using. Store in refrigerator.

Vintage Christmas Stocking Trio

continued from page 15
(also shown on pages 14–15)

2 toe and 2 cuff pieces from those fabrics. Cut an additional 2" w decorative fabric strip for the cuff piece accents.

3. Set the 2 (front and back) stocking pieces right side up on the work surface. Fold under ¼" of the bottom edge of the cuff pieces; iron the folded edge flat. Lay a cuff piece over the top of each stocking piece. Fold under ¼" on the straight side of the toe pieces: iron the folded edges flat. Lay a toe piece over the toe of each stocking piece. Fold under ¼" of the top and bottom of the decorative fabric strip. Iron the folded strip flat.

4. Lay the decorative strip along the bottom edge of the cuff piece. Lay the rickrack or chiffon trim over the bottom edge of the fabric strip. Check the 2 sides of the stocking to make sure the decorative elements line up. Pin everything in place and then machine-stitch the cuff, trims, fabric strip and top edge of the toe piece in place.

5. Placing right sides together, pin the front and the back of the stocking together. Stitch around the outside edge leaving the top open. Turn the stocking right side out.

6. Create a hanging loop by cutting a 1 ½" w by 6" long fabric strip. Fold the strip in half lengthwise and then machine stitch the cut ends together. Turn the strip right side out and press.

7. With right sides together pin the front and back linings together. Machine-stitch around the outside edge, leaving the top open and a 2" opening just above the heel.

8. Attach the lining to the stocking while adding the hanging loop. Slide the stocking into the inside lining. Fold the hanging loop in half, and slip the folded end between the lining and the stocking. Pin the top edges together catching the hanging loop in the pin.

(continued on page 120)

(continued from page 119)

9. Machine-stitch around the top of the stocking. Pull the stocking right side out through the 2" opening in the lining. Hand-stitch the lining opening closed; slide the lining down into the toe. Press.

10. Add die-cut flowers, lace pieces or shell buttons to the front of the stocking if desired.

Silent Night Bedding Trims
continued from page 16
(also shown on page 16)

1. Measure the top sheet, side to side. Cut a strip of checked fabric 6" w x the sheet width measurement plus 2", piecing as needed to make the length.

2. Cut 2" bias strips x sheet width measurement plus 2" for flat flange, piecing as needed to make the length. With wrong sides together, press strips in half lengthwise. Set aside.

3. Cut 1" bias strip x sheet width measurement plus 2" for piping, piecing as needed to make the length. Make piping using zipper foot. Set aside.

4. Press ½" seam on long edge of sheet turn-back strip.

5. To layer elements, pin flat flange to long edge of strip with raw edges even and right sides together. Baste.

6. Repeat step with piping on top of flat flange. Stitch.

7. Lay long strip on sheet with right sides together, making sure to stitch past the sheet turn-back stitching. The strip will be to the left of your needle, then switch back to the right. Stitch close to piping.

8. Turn strip towards top of sheet and press flap to back of sheet. Pin in place so you can stitch in ditch (close to piping) from front, catching the ½" pressed under earlier. **Note:** For a simple option, use iron-on hem tape to adhere to back of sheet turn back.

9. Using matching thread, topstitch the rickrack beside the piping. If desired, gather the flange every 10" and secure with a tack stitch. Sew red buttons to where gathered if desired.

10. Repeat the same process for the pillow case.

Gingham Rickrack Apron
continued from page 18
(also shown on page 18)
floss to couch the rickrack to the apron pocket, starting 4" from the bottom. Press under ¼" on the sides and bottom of the pocket. Press

under ¼" at the top and then 1" to form wide hem. Whipstitch top hem in place. Press. Position pocket on apron front and topstitch to apron at bottom and sides.

5. Press under sides of apron and narrow hem the sides of the apron front. At apron bottom, turn up a 4" hem and machine-stitch in place. Form tucks on apron front and baste in place so top measurement measures 19" in width. With right sides together lay apron waistband and top of apron front together. Pin and stitch. Turn right side out and press under hem at waistband back. Whipstitch in place. Turn back raw edges of waistband at sides.

6. Make apron ties by narrow hemming both sides and one end of each tie. Slide unfinished end of tie into end of sides of waistband. Topstitch in place.

Christmas-Red Cross-Stitch Apron
continued from page 19
(also shown on page 19)

1. From the gingham fabric cut the following pieces:
Cut one 24" long x 30" w piece for the apron front.
Cut two 3½" x 36" pieces for the apron ties.

120

Cut one 4" w x 20" long piece for the apron waistband.
Cut one 6" w x 7½" long piece for the pocket. Press all pieces.

2. Referring to the Cross-Stitch Pattern Grid (page 157) use 3 strands of floss to cross-stitch the apron front starting 7" from the unfinished bottom of the apron front piece. (For Cross-Stitch Diagram, see page 141.) Set aside.

3. Referring to the Cross-Stitch Pattern Grid (page 157) use 3 strands of floss to cross-stitch the apron tie ends, starting 3" from each end. Set aside.

4. Referring to the Cross-Stitch Pattern Grid (page 157) use 3 strands of floss to cross-stitch the apron pocket, starting 4" from the bottom. Press under ¼" on the sides and bottom of the pocket. Press under ¼" at the top and then 1" to form wide hem. Whipstitch top hem in place. Press. Position pocket on apron front and topstitch to apron at bottom and sides.

5. Press under ¼" at sides of apron front and narrow hem. Turn under ¼" and then 5" at apron bottom for hem. Machine stitch in place. Form tucks on apron front and baste in place so top measurement measures 19" in width. With right sides together lay apron waistband and top of apron front together. Pin and stitch. Turn right side out and press under hem at waistband back. Whipstitch in place. Turn back raw edges of waistband at sides.

6. Make apron ties by narrow hemming both sides of each tie. Narrow hem and turn under 2" hem at each cross-stitched tie end and whipstitch in place. Slide unfinished end of tie into end of sides of waistband. Topstitch in place.

Welcoming Apple Basket
continued from page 19
(also shown on page 19)

1. Enlarge and trace scallop pattern (page 146). Use this as a guide for the scallops after the measurements have been taken. Measure the basket length, width and height. To make body of basket liner, take length measurement plus 1" x the front height, width and back height plus 3".

2. Cut 2 pieces for ends of basket liner with measurement of basket width plus 1" x the height plus 2". The liner has a 1" overlap all around the basket.

3. Cut 4 strips of contrast fabric the width of end pieces x 3½" for scallop. Cut notch in center of long side for width of handle.

4. Cut 4 pieces length of body x 3½". Cut 4 long strips 24" x 2" for ties. Press and topstitch. Set aside.

5. Match up 2 of each side with right sides together. Trace scallop on one edge of each. Stitch ¼" away from edge. Clip curves and turn right side out. Press.

6. Pin scallop pieces to body pieces. Stitch ½" seam. Using zipper foot, make piping and insert if desired. Stitch end pieces into body of liner with right sides together. Add ties at each side of handle notches.

7. Finish edges with serger or zig zag stitch if desired. Insert liner wrong side down with scalloped flap folded over edge of basket. Wind ties around handles and tie at top.

Birch Bark-Wrapped Poinsettias
(also shown on page 24)
Pieces of birch bark fall off of the trees in the winter. Use these rich-textured pieces to surround your bright-red poinsettias.

- pieces of natural birch bark
- tall containers to fit inside bark
- ceramic plant saucer
- flat stones
- small sticks
- fresh poinsettias
- fresh greenery

1. Fill the containers with water and set on the ceramic saucer. Wrap the birch bark around the containers.

2. Place poinsettia stems and greenery into the water in the containers. Arrange the rocks and sticks around the bark.

Felt Mushroom Ornaments

continued from page 26
(also shown on page 26)
Cut 2 mushroom caps out of burgundy, pink or brown felt. Cut the cap underside and stem base out of squash or beige felt. Finally, cut the stem piece out of satin.

2. Stack the 2 mushroom cap pieces together. Cut a 5" length of leather cording for a hanging loop. Fold loop in half and tie the ends in an overhand knot. Slip the loop folded end down between the 2 cap pieces. The knot should sit on the center top of the cap. Pin the 2 layers together, then machine stitch the top pieces together. Leave the bottom edges un-sewn.

3. Fold the cap base in half and cut the indicated slits in the center of the circle. Placing right sides together, pin the base to the open bottom of the connected cap.

4. Machine-stitch around the outside edge of the cap. Pull the cap right side out through the slit opening. Hand-stitch button 'spots' around the cap by using a sewing needle and thread to stitch a variety of different sized buttons to the mushroom cap. Hide knots inside cap.

5. Stitch the satin stem to the felt stem base piece. Placing right sides together, line the bottom edge of the satin stem with the edge of the felt base piece. Starting $^1/_4$" from the satin edge, begin machine-stitching the 2 pieces together. As you work your way around the circle, continue to move the satin stem fabric into position. When you've encircled the base, end the seam. (You should have an extra $^1/_4$" of satin left at the beginning and end of the base.) Line up these edges and then machine-stitch them together to form the length of the stem. Begin your seam at the felt base. Trim away excess fabric and turn the stem right side out.

6. Lightly stuff the mushroom stem. Insert the open stem end up into the slit in the base of the mushroom cap. Pin the stem in place. Make small stitches with sewing needle and thread to sew the felt and satin together, leaving the thread attached. Wrap the stem connection with a small section of fringe, pick up the needle and sew the fringe in place.

7. Embroider the edge of the mushroom cap using a full strand of floss and the embroidery needle to blanket stitch around the mushroom cap. (For Blanket-Stitch Diagram see page 140.) Hide your knot under the mushroom fringe, then draw the needle out the edge of the cap. Make

each new blanket stitch $^1/_4$" from the mushroom cap edge. Connect the first and last stitches together, and then bring the needle back out under the fringe to knot the end.

Rickrack Posies

continued from page 30
(also shown on page 29, 30)
1. Unwrap the rickrack from the card and press. Cut the length of rickrack in half. Intertwine the two pieces, layering them side by side. Machine stitch through both pieces catching both pieces on one side of the intertwined pieces. See Photo A.

Photo A

2. Starting at the end, tightly coil the stitched length of rickrack, wrapping the rickrack around and around gluing as you wrap. Continue to coil the rickrack until the wrapped piece looks like a flower bloom shape. Trim end. Glue to secure.

3. Cut the muslin into a small circle. Glue the piece of muslin to the back of the coiled flower to stabilize the wrapped flower.

4. For the pin or hair clip, cut 2 leaf shapes from the wool or silk scrap. Topstitch leaf vein lines through both pieces leaving the raw edges unfinished. Glue to the back of the muslin circle. Sew or glue a hair clip or pin back to the back. See Photo B.

Photo B

5. For the package topper, cut green ribbon into short lengths. Glue the pieces of green ribbon to the back of the muslin. Attach to the package using double-stick tape. See Photo C.

Photo C

Handmade
Note Cards & Holder
continued from page 31
(also shown on page 31)
2. Cut a rectangle of coordinating paper for each card and adhere next to the message.
3. Punch or die-cut shapes such as stars, hearts, snowflakes, trees or ornaments from cardstock and emboss as desired. Adhere a shape to the front of each card using foam dots.
4. Add self-adhesive nail heads or jewels to the cards as desired. Cut a rectangle of cardstock and adhere to the inside of each card. Write desired message on the inside of the card.

For the Plastic Box and Band:
Note: Fill the box with cards and envelopes so that it doesn't bend as you're wrapping the band around it. Check to see how many cards and envelopes your box will hold, based on the thickness of the completed cards.
1. Cut 2 wide strips of paper to wrap around the box, one a bit narrower than the other. Mark and score the paper so that the strips will wrap neatly around the box.
2. Adhere the scored strips together with strong double-sided tape with the cut ends positioned on the bottom side of the plastic box.
3. Punch or die-cut 3 shapes such as trees, snowflakes or ornaments from cardstock. Punch a small hole in each and string on a length of twine or cording. Wrap wide ribbon around the box and tie in a bow. Tie the twine to the ribbon, tucking it under the knot.

Nine-Patch Pot Holder

continued from page 33

(also shown on page 33)

5. Cut a piece of backing fabric 1" larger all around than the pieced block.

6. Sandwich the heat-resistant interfacing between the backing and the finished block. Baste around the edges of the layered pieces. Bind and quilt the block as desired.

7. Make a fabric loop by folding a 1"x3" piece of fabric into a narrow strip. Whipstitch edges closed and tack to corner of pot holder. Sew a button on pot holder at opposite corner.

Needle-Felted Drink Cozies

continued from page 35

(also shown on page 35)

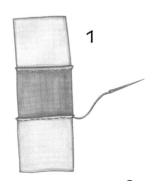

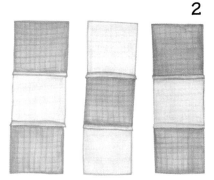

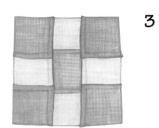

Note: The felting tool connects the two layers of felt without need to sew or glue anything. For tips on needle-felting see page 142.

For the Tea Time Cozy

- 4"x10" piece of fuchsia felt or dimension to fit around chosen glass or mug
- scrap of white felt for tea bag
- one skein each white, red and blue embroidery floss
- scrap of blue felt
- embroidery needle
- needle-felting tool, such as Clover needle-felting tool
- small button
- 3" piece of narrow elastic

For the Tea Time Cozy:

1. Using fabric scissors, cut out a wide fuchsia felt strip to fit around a chosen mug. Cut 2 thin, long strips from light blue felt.

2. Using needle-felting tool, felt the blue strips into the wide fuchsia strip.

3. Using the pattern (page 153) cut a tea bag shape from white felt. Needle-felt the tea bag shape into fuchsia strip. Using embroidery floss in red and blue, embroider the recipient's name onto the tea bag, or a heart shape and the word "tea".

4. Using silver floss, embroider the tea bag's string and star shapes. Sew on button and elastic silver cord to the ends for securing around mug.

For the Christmas Tree Cozy:

1. Using fabric scissors, cut out a wide cream felt strip to fit around a chosen mug. Cut a wavy shape for snow from white felt. Using the pattern (page 153) cut a green tree shape from green felt.

2. Using the needle-felting tool, felt snow shape over the top of the cream felt strip.

3. Repeat the process to connect the green felt tree layer to the cream felt strip. Embroider star shapes and garland on the tree using metallic embroidery floss. Sew on button and elastic silver cord to the ends for securing around mug.

For the Snowman Cozy:
1. Using fabric scissors, cut out a wide light blue felt strip to fit around a chosen mug. Referring to pattern (page 153) cut 2 circles from white felt, larger for snowman's body, smaller for the head. Cut tiny strip of fabric out of an old sweater or other knit fabric for snowman's scarf.
2. Using needle-felting tool, felt the 2 circles to make snowman shape onto light blue strip. Give the snowman eyes using black embroidery floss. Embroider stars using silver embroidery floss.
3. Hot-glue the tiny strip of sweater around snowman's neck to create a scarf. Sew on button and elastic silver cord to the ends for securing around mug.

Framed Button Tree
(also shown on page 37)
Gather together favorite vintage buttons to display in a tree shape for a stunning holiday piece.

- picture frame
- cardboard or thick matte board
- assorted buttons/buckle
- art paper
- scissors
- crafts glue

1. Cut cardboard or thick matte board to fit within a chosen frame. Glue decorative art paper to the cardboard or matte board. (This will keep the paper from warping.) Set aside to dry.
2. Arrange buttons in tree shape on another surface. Use a large rectangular button or belt buckle for the tree trunk. Layer various vintage buttons together. Try to vary the shape, pattern, size and color. Once you have a final design, take a photo of it so you have it for reference when you begin gluing.
3. Transfer and glue the buttons one by one to create the tree design on paper-covered cardboard/matte board. Let dry.
4. Frame the piece in a picture frame with no glass.

Stacked Button Wreath
continued from page 38
(also shown on page 38)
1. Spray the fresh wreath with spray snow. Let dry.
2. Layer the buttons as desired using hot glue to secure. Tuck the buttons into the wreath using wire to secure if necessary.

3. Tie a bow using the checked ribbon, sliding the ribbon through the belt buckle. Attach at the top of the wreath.

Colorful Circle Garland
(also shown on page 38)
A simple strand of felt circles instantly adds homespun charm to your mantle or tree. Die-cutting machines speed the assembly process, allowing you to create a lengthy garland in record time. Play with color, shape and buttons to create vibrant variety.

- buttons in assorted colors of green, red and white
- wool felt such as National Nonwovens in dark and light green, red and white.
- embroidery floss in white and red
- red sewing thread
- 1/2" red ribbon in desired length
- flower and circle dies such as Sizzix Big Kick (optional)
- scissors
- embroidery floss
- embroidery needle
- hot-glue gun and glue sticks

1. Using a die-cut machine or with scissors, cut the desired number of circles measuring $2^{1}/2$", 2", $1^{3}/4$", $1^{1}/2$", $1^{1}/4$" and 1". Or, use the patterns provided (page 149).

(continued on page 126)

(continued from page 125)

Each circle on the garland features 6 circles; 2 large, 2 medium and 2 small.

2. Arrange circles into stacked pairs. The garland is 2-sided so each circle has 2 fronts that sandwich the ribbon. Stack the felt elements together largest to smallest, mixing colors and shapes; then top each stack with a button.

3. Sew the buttons to the center of the stack. Thread an embroidery needle with a full strand of floss, bring the needle up through the layers of circles and stitch the button to the felt.

4. Embroider the edges of the circles by using contrasting floss to make decorative stitches around the circles. We used the blanket-stitch and the running-stitch. (See pages 140–142 for Stitch Diagrams.) Hide your knots on the underside.

5. Plan the design by spreading the sewn pairs across the work surface. Alternate the colors and sizes so that the garland will be variegated and interesting. Hot-glue the backs of the pairs together trapping the ribbon in between. Position the circles 3" apart.

6. Add buttons to the garland between the felt circles. Use a sewing needle and red thread so that your stitches camouflage with the ribbon.

Friendly Owls

continued from page 39
(also shown on page 39)
owl, one front and another for the back. Cut the head and wing patterns out of felt that won't fray. For added embellishment, trim the inside edge of the wings with pinking sheers. Cut pairs of circle eye pieces out of the felt and wool scraps.

2. Sew the head piece to the top of the front body piece. Position the head over the top of the front body and the wings against either side. Machine-stitch the bottom edge of the head and the inside edge of the wings to the body.

3. Stitch the front and back body pieces together by placing right sides together. Lay the back body piece over the front. Pin and machine stitch the 2 pieces together. Begin and end the seam at the wing leaving a 1½" opening. Check that the felt wing and head pieces have been caught in your seam. Trim away the excess fabric at the ears and turn the owl right side out.

4. Stuff the owl by pushing stuffing into the owl's ears first. Then fill the rest of the body. Layer the eye circles largest to smallest over the head piece. Try different colored circles and buttons together until you find the ideal arrangement. Use a contrasting color thread to sew the eyes in place. Insert the sewing needle through the opening in the wing, then draw it up through the center of the circles and into the button. Bring it back down through the second button hole. Once you've stitched both eyes in place, knot your threads under the last eye circle.

5. Embroider the breast feathers by embellishing the solid wool breast with cross-stitch feathers. (For Cross Stitch Diagram, see page 141.) Using an embroidery needle and a full strand of embroidery floss, bring the needle in through the opening in the wing and begin making 4 diagonal stitches spaced about ½" apart under the eyes. Work your way back across, completing the stitches by crossing them in the opposite direction. Make a second line of 3 stitches in the negative spaces below the first. Repeat for desired number of feathers.

Winter-White Button Bracelet and Earrings

continued from page 40
(also shown on page 40)
4. Once the chain is filled with button dangles, attach the lobster clasp. Use both your round and chain nose pliers to open the jump ring laterally. Link the clasp and last link of the chain onto the jump ring. Close the ring with the pliers until you hear and feel it spring back into shape.

For the Earrings
1. Choose small buttons for the earrings. Select 4 pairs of matching buttons that measure $3/4"$, $1/2"$ and two $1/4"$ pairs. Separate them into 2 groupings arranging them largest to smallest. Then place the second small pair on top.

2. Link together the buttons with jump rings. Use both round and chain nose pliers to open a jump ring laterally. Link the first 2 buttons onto the jump ring. Close the ring with the pliers until you hear and feel it spring back into shape. Repeat the process with new jump rings to connect the second button to the third button, and then again to connect the third button to the fourth button.

3. Hook the ear wires through the top buttons. Open the bottom of the ear wires laterally with chain nose pliers. Link the open ear wire through the top button and then bend the ear wire back into shape.

Snowflake and Tree Button Cards

continued from page 41
(also shown on page 41)
3. Stamp your message first. Test stamp on scrap paper first. Lay the background paper on your note card for placement then stamp your message below it. **Note:** By stamping your message first, you can avoid finishing a card only to ruin it with a stamping error at the end.

4. Glue on the paper pieces. Use a light application of glue stick to position the backgrounds, tree and tree base or 4 circles. (Too much glue will make it hard to sew.)

5. Plan the placement of the buttons. **For the tree,** place a white button at the top of the tree and 7 red buttons over the triangle. **For the snowflake,** place a white button in the center of each of the snowflake circles. Place 4 additional buttons outside of the circles. Make a mental note of the best arrangement and then move them aside.

6. To attach the buttons on the card, **for the tree card,** thread the sewing needle with three strands of silver floss; tie the end into a knot. Beginning at the top of the tree, bring the needle from the back of the paper to the front. Stitch the white button to the top of the tree, by poking the needle back through to the back side. Bring the needle back out the front of the card about $1/2"$ down from the first button. This time attach a red button.

7. Continue working in this fashion attaching the 6 remaining red buttons to the tree. At this point the silver thread will only be seen inside the buttons on the front cover. The stitches are all on the back side of the cover.

8. To add embroidery floss garland to the tree, simply make diagonal stitches across the front of the tree. Make some long stitches that span the entire width, then intersperse them with smaller stitches that only reach as far as a button.

(continued on page 128)

(continued from page 127)

9. For the snowflake card, thread sewing needle with three strands of off-white floss, then tie the end into a knot. Begin with the biggest circle, bring the needle from the back of the cover out the front. Stitch a button to the center of the circle, poke the needle back through to the back side.
10. Repeat the process to attach a button to the center of the 3 smaller circles, and then sew 4 buttons outside of the circles. At this point the white thread will only be seen inside the buttons on the front cover, the stitches are all on the back side of the cover.
11. To add decorative snowflake stitches to a plain button, simply make a long cross stitch that slips under the button. Then intersect it with a second cross stitch with slightly smaller stitches. Even though you made just 4 stitches, the button will appear to have 4 long and 4 short stitches that emerge from the sides. Repeat the process with the 3 remaining buttons.
Note: Remember once you've made a hole with a needle it can't be undone. Be careful where you poke. Always begin and end your threads on the backside of the cover.

Picture-Perfect Gift Wrap
(also shown on page 43)
Don't leave those adorable photos in a box! Photocopy them and use them as paper ribbon to adorn your holiday gifts.

• box to wrap
• wrapping paper in plain and printed colors
• desired photos
• large sheet of white paper
• copy machine or scanner
• ribbon
• double-stick tape
• transparent tape
• crafts glue
• scissors

1. Wrap the box in desired paper being sure to crease the sides of the paper when wrapping. Set aside.
2. Using the size of the wrapped box as a guide for size, lay the photos on the white paper in a horizontal row, temporarily securing with double-stick tape. Copy the photos on a copy machine. Cut out the photos.
3. Lay the photos on the box in desired pattern. Slide the ribbon behind the photos for a border effect. Glue the ribbon in place. Place the photos on top of the ribbon and use double-stick tape to secure.

Paper Poppers
(also shown on page 44)
Simple cardboard rolls turn into little presents for each guest at the table.

• cardboard paper towel rolls
• lightweight wrapping paper
• scissors
• pencil
• crafts glue
• narrow ribbon
• small candies or presents for inside the poppers

1. Cut paper towel roll to measure about 6" in length. Mark the center of the 6" roll and cut in half.
2. Cut a 7"x12" piece of wrapping paper. Put the 2 roll pieces back together, butting edges together. Roll the wrapping paper around the 2 pieces, leaving extra paper at both ends. Secure at the back with crafts glue. Let dry.
3. Slide the candies and little presents into the roll from one end. Squeeze the paper at each end and tie with a piece of ribbon. Trim ends.
4. To open, snap the popper and it will pop and open where the 2 pieces were put back together.

Garland of Greetings
(also shown on page 45)
Much-loved Christmas cards are recycled to make a holiday greeting.

- old Christmas cards
- alphabet letter stickers
- paper punch
- scissors
- narrow ribbon
- 2 small jingle bells

1. Cut the fronts from the Christmas cards. Choose cards with interesting fronts and open areas for the letters.
2. Punch a hole in each upper corner of the cards.
3. Position the adhesive alphabet letters to spell holiday words.
4. Thread the ribbon through the holes at the top of the card to hang. Tie a jingle bell towards the ends of the ribbon.

Felt Candy Wreath
continued from page 50
(also shown on page 50)

1. Using a cutting mat, straight edge and rotary cutter, cut all shades of pink and white felt into a generous pile of 1" w strips. Try to maximize the available length. 18" long strips are ideal. 12" or smaller lengths can be used to roll smaller felt candies.
2. Select a white strip and pink strip that are approximately the same length. Fold the very end of each piece in half. Pinch the 2 folded ends together. Begin rolling them into a spiral. Continue to fold the length of the strips as you roll them. Once you reach the end of the strip, trim the inner strip so the end tucks under the outer strip. Use a straight pin to hold the ends flat.
3. Continue rolling the felt candies until you have approximately 40 pieces. You'll need approximately 13 large felt candies that are each 2" to 2 ³/₄" diameter for the front of the wreath, and 27 smaller felt candies that are 1 ¹/₄" to 2" diameter to cover the inside and outside of the wreath edges.
4. Using hot glue and working with a single felt candy piece at a time,

remove the straight pin, and glue the strip ends to secure. Glue the inside strip end first then glue the outer strip over it. To stabilize the center of the candies, scribble a few lines of hot glue across the wrong side (the cut edge side). Work your way through all the felt candies, until they're all unpinned, glued and stabilized.
5. Arrange the finished felt candies on the wreath by placing large felt candies over the front of the wreath and smaller ones around the inside and outside of the wreath. Use the smallest felt candies to fill in holes.
6. Once you're pleased with the arrangement, begin gluing individual felt candies in place. Apply a generous amount of glue to the backside of each felt candy. Use a straight pin to hold the glued felt candy against the foam while the glue sets.
Note: If you use pins without plastic heads, you can press the pins deeply into the center of the felt candies and leave them in place after the glue sets.

Sweet Chair Back Slip
continued from page 52
(also shown on page 52)

- ¼ yard of pink striped fabric for piping
- 1 yard of ¼" cording for piping
- 1 red button
- matching sewing thread
- sewing machine
- scissors
- candy cane
- fresh greenery

1. Measure chair back. Enlarge, adjust and trace pattern (page 152) onto tracing paper. Cut front and back pieces from the striped fabric, adjusting for length and width of your chair.
2. Make piping with bias cut strips from pink striped fabric. Pipe scalloped edges of piece. With right sides together, lay facing over front; pin, matching all curves and edges.
3. Stitch all around perimeter of piece, leaving openings for turning. Turn and press. Whipstitch or hem tape openings closed.
4. Cut a 5"x 8" piece of polka-dot fabric for pocket. Fold in half and press, turning under sides and top. Open and topstitch the top

of pocket. Refold with wrong sides facing, and whipstitch sides leaving a 1" opening for ties. Sew a button to the front of the pocket.
5. Cut 2 strips of polka-dot fabric 3" x the length needed to tie around the chair. Narrow hem edges. Slide through side pocket holes. Lay the chair cover over the chair back and tie the pocket around chair.
6. Place fresh greenery and candy cane in pocket.

Candy Jar Table Favor
(also shown on page 53)
Everyone will love the little sweetness you give them in their own personalized jar.

- small canning jar
- ½" w red-and-white striped ribbon
- ¼" w pink ribbon
- double-stick tape
- scissors
- alphabet stickers
- snowflake sticker
- peppermint candies, lollipops and candy canes

1. Be sure the jar is clean and dry. Wrap the ribbon around the jar top, crisscrossing at the front. Secure with double-stick tape.

2. Cut a small piece of the pink ribbon and lay flat on table. Adhere the snowflake and a letter to the middle of the ribbon. Use double-stick tape to adhere the ribbon where the ribbon crosses.
3. Fill the jar with peppermint candies, lollipops and candy canes.

Peppermint Pinwheel Table Runner
continued from page 54
(also shown on pages 54–55)

From white-on-white print fabric cut:
One 14¼" square. Cut square in half diagonally in both directions.
Six 5⅜" squares. Cut each square in half diagonally.

From green-and-white print fabric cut:
Two 2½" w x 33" long rectangles.
Two 2½" w x 13" long rectangles.
Two 2½" w x 11" long rectangles.

Assembling the Quilt Center

1. Working with the pink-and-white stripe triangles and the same size white print triangles, join each stripe triangle to a white print triangle along the long diagonal edge. See Diagram 1.

Diagram 1

2. Join 4 triangle-squares to make a pinwheel square. Repeat with remaining triangle-squares. See Diagram 2.

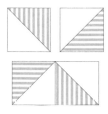

Diagram 2

2. Repeat, working with the pink-and-white dotted triangles and the same size white print triangles, join each pink triangle to a white triangle along the long diagonal edge. Join 4 triangle-squares to make a pinwheel square.

3. Join pinwheel squares and large white triangles. The white triangles are slightly larger. See Diagram 3.

Diagram 3

4. Trim sides to $1/4$" beyond points of outside edges of pinwheels. See Diagram 4.

Diagram 4

5. Join one green print $2 1/2$"x11" rectangle to one right side of each point; trim even with long sides. Join one $2 1/2$"x13" rectangle to adjacent side of each point; trim even with long sides. See Diagram 5.

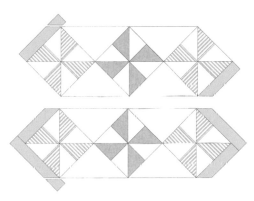

Diagram 5

6. Add one green print $2 1/2$"x 33" rectangle to each long side; trim even with the end borders. See Diagram 6.

Diagram 6

Finishing the quilt

1. Layer the quilt top, batting and backing.

2. Quilt in the ditch through the centers of the pinwheels and then as desired.

3. Trim excess batting and backing.

4. Join together the pink dotted $2 1/4$" w strips with diagonal seams to make a continuous strip. Use to bind the quilt.

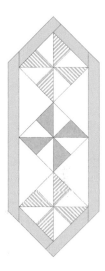

Finished Quilt

Candy-Striped Cones

continued from page 56
(also shown on page 56)

1. Trace pattern (page 153) onto tracing paper and cut out. Trace around pattern onto scrapbook paper and cut out.

2. Curve paper around to form cone. Glue along paper edge and secure temporarily with the close pin. Let dry. Remove clothespin.

3. Glue ribbon at the top edge of the cone. Let dry. Make a hole on each side of the cone using the awl.

4. Knot one end of the narrow ribbon. Starting from the outside, thread through the hole to the other side. Pull ribbon out and knot on the outside of the other hole. Adjust ribbon. Fill with candy.

Clock Collection Holiday Display

(also shown on page 59)
Vintage clocks keep time with newer timepieces when they are combined for a holiday arrangement. Group the clocks on the rungs of a ladder or on a mantel. Put some clocks in front of each other mixing and matching colors, sizes and shapes. Tuck fresh evergreen and holly around the clocks for sure-to-be timely conversation starter.

Quick Felt Stockings

(also shown on page 60)
Felt comes in all colors and textures, and even with its own eyelet trim. First, make a simple stocking and trim it with a running stitch. Then finish it with a lovely cuff using purchased eyelet trim.

- tracing paper
- pencil
- scissors
- 13" piece of felt for each stocking
- 7" strip of purchased eyelet felt for cuffs
- $3/8$" x 6" strip of felt for loop
- embroidery floss

1. Enlarge stocking pattern (page 152) and cut out. Cut patterns from appropriate fabrics, cutting front and back from felt and cuff from eyelet fabric, making sure that the eyelet design is at the bottom of the cuff pattern. Mark toe and heel stitching lines.

2. Using the running stitch, stitch lines on stocking fronts using 6 strands of embroidery floss. (For Running Stitch Diagram, see page 142.)

3. Sew stocking pieces with right sides together, using $1/4"$ seam, leaving top straight edge open. Clip curves.

4. Fold loop in half and baste to upper back edge of stocking on lining side.

5. Stitch short ends of cuff, right sides together. Pin right side of cuff to wrong side of stocking. Stitch with $1/4"$ seam. Turn cuff to outside, turning stocking right side out. Press lightly.

Punched Luminarias

continued from page 61
(also shown on page 61)

1. Cut the top of the bag off to get desired height.

2. Decide where pattern is to be on the paper bag. Use the paper punch to make the shapes. If larger shapes are desired, place a piece of cardboard between the front and back of bag and mark design. Cut out using crafts knife.

3. Place glass container with votive candle in bag.

Never leave a burning candle unattended.

Holiday Bolster Pillows

(also shown on page 61)
Dress up that easy chair for the holidays with brightly colored bolster pillows made using purchased kitchen towels.

- purchased small bolster pillow form
- purchased kitchen towel
- ribbon
- scissors
- matching sewing thread
- needle

1. Press towel and lay on flat surface. Lay pillow form in center of towel. Wrap towel around the form. See Diagram 1.

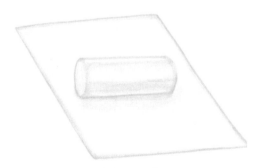

Diagram 1

2. Using the running stitch, secure with small stitches on back. (For Running Stitch Diagram, see page 142.) See Diagram 2.

Diagram 2

3. Gather ends of towel and tie with ribbon to secure. Clip ends of ribbon. See Diagram 3.

Diagram 3

small hole with a ½" circle punch. Adhere the reinforcements around the holes in the paper strips.

2. Use brown ink to distress the edges of the paper and cardstock.

3. Place bread in plastic before adding the band if desired. Place the strips around the bread and determine the appropriate length for each strip. Trim each strip and tape together in the middle (which will be on the bottom side of the loaf). Thread twine/jute through the holes and tie at the top.

Paper Band & Tag
(also shown on page 65)
• tracing paper
• pencil
• scissors
• adhesive, including foam dots, tape adhesive, and small glue dots or liquid glue
• small hole punch
• ½" circle punch
• brown ink for distressing edges of paper
• cardstock patterned paper for wrap
• cardstock in 3 coordinating colors for tag base, heart, and text strip
• jute and/or twine in coordinating colors
• small button

For the Band:
1. Cut two 2½x12" strips of patterned paper. Cut the corners off of one end of each strip to resemble a tag. Use the small hole punch to make a hole in each strip. **Tip:** Create your own hole reinforcements by punching a small hole in coordinating cardstock. Then punch around the

For the Tag:
1. Copy the tag and heart pattern pieces (page 144) onto cardstock and cut out. Punch a small hole in the top of the tag. Use brown ink to distress the edges of the cardstock before adhering pieces. Adhere the heart to the tag using foam pop dots. Create and cut out the text strip and adhere across the heart.

2. Thread twine through small button and knot. Adhere the button with a small glue dot or liquid glue. Tie the tag to the wrap using twine or jute.

Christmas Cupcake Boxes
(also shown on pages 66–68)
• pre-made cupcake boxes (available at crafts and office supply stores)
• 12"x12" cardstock and patterned paper
• scissors
• ½" and ¼" circle punch for tag
• small corner rounder for tag
• ribbon for attaching tag to box
• holly leaf die-cut or punch
• red glitter glue such as Stickles (optional)
• strong tape adhesive, double-sided tape sheets or liquid glue
• circle punch (approximately 1½") for adhering rosettes
• scoring board and scoring tool
• embellishments for rosettes such as buttons, ribbon, tulle or monogram stamp
• scalloped or circle dies in graduated sizes

1. Cut paper/cardstock to fit around sides of box and lid. Use a scoring tool for crisp corners. Add a band of paper/cardstock around the center of the box for trim. Add rosettes to the top of the box (see instructions below) and trim as desired.

To Make Rosettes:
1. Cut a strip of paper or cardstock 12" long and at least 1¼" wide.

(The width of your paper will determine the size of the rosette. The completed rosette will be twice the width of your strip.)

2. Using a scoring board, make score lines along the strip at ¼" increments. Accordion fold the strip on the score lines. Adhere the ends of the strip together to form a ring using a strong tape adhesive. Punch a circle from cardstock to help secure the rosette. Apply strong tape adhesive or liquid glue to one side of the punched circle and set aside for a moment.

3. Gently push down on the center of the accordion-folded strip to press it flat. It should now look like a rosette. Position the rosette onto the glued punched circle and hold in place. Place a heavy object (such as a glue bottle) on top of the rosette while it dries.

Note: You can create rosettes in graduated sizes and layer them on top of each other. Other ideas for topping a rosette: Layer with scalloped circles, attach a button with twine, tulle or ribbon. Top with a stamped or printed monogram letter or attach a Christmas greeting.

For the Tag:

1. Cut a 2"x3" piece of cardstock for tag base. Round corners. Create tag with name of cupcake onto white cardstock and cut out leaving white background in place. Adhere to center of tag. Trim tag with narrow strips of patterned paper.

2. Punch a ½" circle from cardstock and adhere to the top of the tag to create a reinforcement. Punch a ¼" hole through the circle for ribbon. Optional: Attach die-cut or punched holly leaves to the tag. Add dots of glitter glue to create berries; allow to dry. Thread ribbon through hole in tag and attach to box under rosette.

Candy Box

(also shown on page 69)
- small shallow box with lid
- trimmer
- scissors
- scalloped circles in two large sizes
- ½" circle punch
- scoring blade
- ribbon
- adhesive, including strong tape adhesive and foam dots
- patterned paper and cardstock

1. Measure box and cover outside and inside with patterned paper and cardstock as desired. Place strong tape adhesive around the edge of the box lid, then adhere ribbon.

2. Make dividers for box by cutting strips of cardstock the same depth as the box base. Cut wide slits in each strip and interlock them. (We cut four 6" strips of cardstock, then made wide slits at 2" and 4".)

3. Cut a wide strip of coordinating cardstock to fit across the box lid. Cut 2 scalloped circles from cardstock and adhere to the strip with foam dots.

4. Make a label on white cardstock and cut out. Make 2 score lines on either side of the text, then fold text strip like a banner. Use scissors to notch the ends, then adhere to the top of the box using foam dots. Punch two ½" circles from coordinating cardstock and adhere to either side of the label.

Brown Paper Wrap

(also shown on page 70)
- scissors
- adhesive, including foam dots and strong double-sided tape
- kraft paper (available as wrapping paper in rolls)
- 2 coordinated patterned papers
- cardstock to match patterned papers
- circle punches in 2 sizes
- scalloped circle die or punch to coordinate with circle punches
- glitter pen

For the Cone:

1. Cut a 7¼" square of kraft paper. Place paper on table in front of you, positioned like a diamond shape.

2. Fold the two sides in to create a cone, then fold the remaining point down over the cone. Use strong tape adhesive to adhere the sides.

For the Tag:

1. Cut a 1¼"x 5" strip of patterned paper. Use scissors to cut a notch in one end, creating a banner. Adhere the banner to the top of the cone.

2. Use a circle punch to punch around a design from patterned paper.

Note: Use any paper with a Christmas image, or substitute a sticker or stamped image.

(continued on page 136)

(continued from page 135)

3. Mat the punched image onto a larger punched cardstock circle, then onto a larger scalloped circle cut from cardstock. Use a glitter pen to highlight the punched image. Allow to dry, then adhere the scalloped piece to the banner with foam dots. Create the tag artwork onto cardstock. Cut out and mat on coordinated color, then adhere to the banner. After filling with caramels, adhere the banner piece to the cone.

Parchment Cookie Sleeve

(also shown on page 71)

- parchment paper
- scissors
- piercing tool
- border punch
- small hole punch
- ½" circle punch
- needle
- narrow red-striped twine
- small button
- ribbon

For the Sleeve:

1. Measure the cookie cutter you'll be using to determine the size of envelope needed. Cut a strip of parchment and fold it so that the opening will be at the top.
2. Make holes with a piercing tool along the two sides of the envelope. Use needle and twine to sew a running stitch along the sides of the envelope. (See Running Stitch Diagram, page 142.) Knot on the back side. Use paper to create a narrow border strip along the top edge of the envelope.
3. Trim with a border punched from cardstock. Add a button tied with twine to embellish the envelope.

For the Tag:

1. Trace the tag pattern (page 144) onto white cardstock and cut out. Trace tag outline onto desired paper/cardstock and cut out.
2. Adhere "For You" to the tag, adding strips of paper for decoration. Adhere a ½" circle punched from cardstock to the top of the tag, then punch a hole in the tag with a small hole punch. Thread tag with ribbon and tie/attach to envelope as desired.

Holiday Pretzel Container

(also shown on page 72)

- small oatmeal container
- fine-tip marker
- scissors
- small hole punch for tag
- adhesive, including liquid glue, foam dots, and strong double-sided tape
- border punch
- patterned paper/cardstock
- baker's twine for tag
- tree, snowflake or other Christmas punch for tag
- small jewels or enamel dots to embellish tag and container

For Container:

1. Measure container and cut paper to fit. Place double-sided tape on the back of the paper and carefully adhere to the container.
2. Add strips of patterned paper and cardstock around the bottom and top edge as trim.
3. Use border punch to create an additional strip and layer it over the cardstock trim.
4. Adhere jewels or enamel dots to container as desired using small dots of liquid glue.

For the Tag:

1. Trace circle patterns, page 145, onto light and dark cardstock and cut out on lines. Adhere the circles together, then punch a small hole at the top. Use marker to highlight dotted lines.
2. Adhere punched tree design to tag using foam dots. Embellish with jewels or enamel dots.
3. Thread twine through the tag, then tape the end to the inside of the container. Use a dot of adhesive to adhere the back of the tag to the box in the desired position.

For the Canister:

1. Measure the canister and cut a band of paper to fit around it. Place double-sided tape on the back of the paper and carefully adhere to the jar.
2. Punch borders strips from cardstock and adhere behind a coordinated patterned paper. Adhere to the jar using double-sided tape.
3. Using double-sided tape, adhere a band of ribbon around the jar as trim. Create the tag artwork onto cardstock; cut out and mat on matching cardstock. Add a dot of glitter glue to the center of the snowflakes on the tag; allow to dry. Adhere the tag to the front of the jar using foam dots.

For the Gingerbread Man:

1. Trace or copy gingerbread man pattern (page 145) onto brown cardstock and cut out. Ink the edges of the gingerbread man with brown ink to add dimension and shading.
2. Use a white pen to outline the gingerbread shape and add facial features. Tie a twine bow around the gingerbread man's neck. Punch two small circles from cardstock for buttons and adhere to body. Add dots of glitter glue for sparkle.

Sweet Gift Jar
(also shown on page 74)

- canning jar
- vintage spoon
- ribbon for attaching spoon and tag
- trimmer
- circle cutter or punch
- scissors
- small stapler
- adhesive, including foam dots and strong double-sided tape
- tag die or punch
- hot-glue gun and glue sticks
- small flower die or punch (optional)
- cardstock and patterned paper for paper bow and tag

Note: Lightweight cardstock or paper will work best for creating the loops of the tag.

Creamer Mix Jar
(also shown on page 73)

- tracing paper
- pencil
- square canister-style jar
- trimmer
- scissors
- adhesive, including strong double-sided tape and foam dots
- border punch
- small circle punch for buttons
- patterned paper and cardstock
- narrow ribbon
- twine
- glitter glue such as Stickles
- brown ink for edging gingerbread man
- white pen

For Lid:

1. Cut and adhere narrow strips of paper/cardstock around the edge of the lid using heavy double-sided tape.
2. Use circle cutter or punch to cut paper circle(s) to cover the top of the jar. **Tip:** Create the bow then glue it to the lid after the jar is filled and the lid is closed.

(continued on page 138)

(continued from page 137)

To Make Paper Bow:

1. Create the paper ribbon artwork for the paper bow onto cardstock by writing names of favorite ice creams in lines. Cut 2 strips 8" long, 2 strips 7" long and 2 strips 6" long. (Exact size may be adjusted to fit the size of your jar lid.) Fold each strip into a loop and staple at the center.

2. Criss-cross the 2 longest strips and use hot glue to secure. Do the same with the next two layers. Cut and glue a separate loop for the center of the bow.

For the Tag:

1. Die-cut or punch a tag. Cover a portion of the tag with coordinated paper/cardstock.

2. Create the tag artwork onto contrasting cardstock and cut out. Adhere to the front of the tag using foam dots. Die-cut or punch a small flower from contrasting cardstock if desired. Cut and adhere behind the tag label so that only a portion of it is visible.

3. Wrap a long piece of ribbon around the jar and knot. Tie around the spoon handle, then thread tag onto ribbon and complete the knot. Trim the ribbon.

Note: Fudge sauce should be refrigerated until ready to give or ready to use.

Striped Package Tag
(also shown on page 75)

- tracing paper
- pencil
- trimmer
- scissors
- adhesive, including liquid glue and foam dots
- small hole punch
- ½" circle punch
- small letter stamps to create "for you" text
- stamping ink
- large circle punch to fit stamped text (sample measures 1³⁄₈")
- scalloped circle punch or die, slightly larger than circle punch
- ribbon in coordinating color
- twine in coordinating color
- fine-tipped pen

1. Trace the tag pattern (page 144) onto cardstock or paper and cut out. Make a reinforcement for the tag hole by punching a ½" circle and adhering to the top of the tag. Then punch a hole in the tag through the circle. Cut strips of patterned paper and cardstock to cover the lower portion of the tag.

2. Stamp "for you" and punch out using large circle punch. Mat on

scalloped circle cut or punched from a contrasting color. Use fine-tipped pen to make small decorative dots around the edge of the punched circle.

3. Wrap twine around the tag 2-3 times and tie in a small bow. Adhere the scalloped text piece next to the bow using foam dots. Adjust the position of the bow, then secure with a tiny dot of liquid glue. Thread ribbon through hole in tag and tie to cellophane cookie bag.

Merry Christmas Wrap
(also shown on page 76)

- cellophane bag for popcorn balls
- scissors
- small corner rounder
- adhesive, including liquid glue
- small hole punch
- ½" circle punch
- white cardstock for tag base and text strip
- patterned paper for bottom of tag
- ribbon in coordinating colors
- twine
- small jingle bells
- small button
- fine-tipped glitter glue such as Stickles

1. Create the tag artwork onto white cardstock and cut out. Use small corner rounder on the 4 corners of the tag base. Punch a small hole in the top for ribbon.

2. Cut a small piece of patterned paper to cover the bottom portion of the tag. Adhere the text strip to the center of the tag, extending slightly off either side. Wrap twine around the lower portion of the tag and tie in a small bow. Secure the bow with a tiny dot of liquid glue.

3. Place a dot of glitter glue on either side of "Merry". Allow to dry. Thread the jingle bells onto to the ribbon and through the tag. Tie to the popcorn ball's cellophane bag.

Basket Tag

(also shown on page 77)

- basket
- trimmer
- scissors
- adhesive, including foam dots
- small circle punch (³/4" or 1")
- scoring blade
- cardstock for tag base; contrasting color for accent
- lighter color cardstock for text
- hole punch/eyelet setter and matching eyelets

- ribbon to wrap around bag
- fine tipped paint, such as Liquid Pearls or self-adhesive gems
- Christmas greenery and floral wire or double-sided tape

1. Cut a rectangle from cardstock to fit the front of basket. Use a circle punch to notch the corners. Set eyelets on the two outside edges of the tag base. **Note:** Eyelets are decorative and functional: They will reinforce the ribbon holes in your tag, keeping them from tearing.

2. Create the text onto a lighter color of cardstock and cut out. Make 2 score lines on each side of the text, then bend to create a banner. Use scissors to notch the ends of the text strip. Cut a slightly larger mat using contrasting cardstock. Adhere the mat and the text to the tag base using foam dots under the center portion of the text.

3. Thread the ribbon through the eyelets, wrapping around the back of the basket to secure the tag in place. Tie additional ribbon at the sides of the tag and trim. Place a dot of fine-tipped paint or self-adhesive gems on either side of the text; allow to dry. Wire or tape in place inside the basket.

Snack Mix Jar

(also shown on page 77)

- large jar with panels
- trimmer
- scissors
- small corner rounder
- adhesive, including double-sided tape, liquid glue and foam dots
- coordinated patterned paper and cardstock
- ribbon to fit around edge of lid
- circle cutter
- snowflake die-cut, sticker or punch
- small jewels

1. To decorate the lid, cut a cardstock circle to cover the top of the lid and adhere. Cut a slightly smaller circle from patterned paper and adhere to top of the cardstock. Wrap double-sided tape around the edge of the lid, then adhere ribbon to the tape; trim.

2. Measure the panels on the jar, then cut and cover each with a piece of patterned paper cut to fit. Round corners if suggested by the design of the jar. Create jar label artwork onto cardstock; round corners and adhere to front panel.

3. Adhere small snowflake (punch, die-cut or sticker) to the upper portion of the label with small foam dots. Adhere the gems to center of the snowflake using small dots of liquid glue.

General Instructions

Making Patterns

When the entire pattern is shown, place tracing or tissue paper over the pattern and draw over the lines. For a more durable pattern, use a permanent marker to draw over the pattern on stencil plastic—this is sometimes also called a template.

When only half of the pattern is shown (indicated by a dotted line on the pattern), fold the tracing paper in half. Place the fold along the dotted line and trace the pattern half. Turn the folded paper over and draw over the traced lines on the remaining side. Unfold the pattern and cut it out.

Sizing Patterns

To change the size of the pattern, divide the desired height or width of the pattern (whichever is greater) by the actual height or width of the pattern. Multiply the result by 100 and photocopy the pattern at this percentage.

For example: You want your pattern to be 8"h, but the pattern on the page is 6"h. So 8:6=1.33x100=133%. Copy the pattern at 133%.

If your copier doesn't enlarge to the size you need, enlarge the pattern to the maximum percentage on the copier. Then repeat step 1, dividing the desired size by the size of the enlarged pattern. Multiply this result by 100 and photocopy the enlarged pattern at the new percentage.

For very large projects, you'll need to enlarge the design in sections onto separate sheets of paper. Repeat as needed to reach the desired size and tape the pattern pieces together.

Transferring Patterns to Fabrics

Trace the pattern onto tissue paper. Pin the tissue paper to the felt or fabric and stitch through the paper. Carefully tear the tissue paper away.

TRANSFERRING PATTERNS TO CARDSTOCK OR OTHER MATERIALS

Trace the pattern onto tracing paper. Place the pattern on the cardstock (or whatever material you are transferring to) and use a pencil to lightly draw around the pattern. For pattern details, slip transfer paper between the pattern and the cardstock and draw over the detail lines.

Cutting a Stencil

Enlarge the pattern if necessary. Using a fine-point permanent marker, trace the pattern onto stencil plastic or mylar. Carefully cut the plastic with scissors or a crafts knife, making sure all edges are smooth.

Making a Fabric Circle

Matching right sides, fold the fabric square in half from top to bottom and again from left to right. Tie one end of a length of string to a water-soluble marking pen; insert a thumbtack through the string at the length indicated in the project instructions. Insert the thumbtack through the folded corner of the fabric. Holding the tack in place and keeping the string taut, mark the cutting line (Fig. 1).

Fig. 1

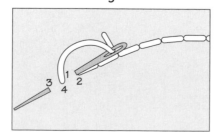

Embroidery Stitches

Always come up at 1 and all odd numbers and go down at 2 and all even numbers unless otherwise indicated.

BACKSTITCH

Bring the needle up at 1, go down at 2, come up at 3 and go down at 4 (Fig. 2).

Fig. 2

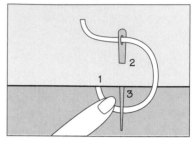

BLANKET STITCH

Referring to Fig. 3, bring the needle up at 1. Keeping the thread below the point of the needle, go down at 2 and come up at 3. Continue working as shown in Fig. 4.

Fig. 3

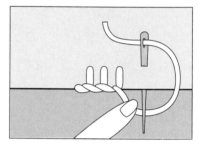

Fig. 4

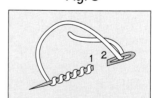

BULLION KNOT

Referring to Fig. 5, bring the needle up at 1 and take the needle down at 2 (this is the distance the knot will cover); come up at 1 again and wrap the yarn around the needle as many times as necessary to cover the distance between 1 and 2. Pull needle through wraps and adjust on the 1-2 loop (Figs. 6-7).

Fig. 5

Fig. 6

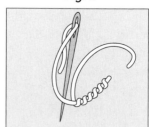

Anchor the knot with a small straight stitch at 2 (Fig. 8).

Fig. 7

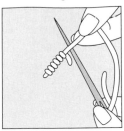

Fig. 8

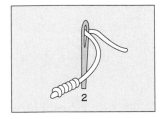

CHAIN STITCH

Referring to Fig. 9, bring the needle up at 1; take the needle down again at 1 to form a loop. Bring the needle up at 2; take the needle down again at 2 to form a second loop (Fig. 10). Continue making loops. Anchor the last chain with a small straight stitch (Fig. 11).

Fig. 9

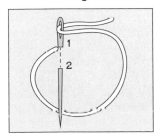

Fig. 10

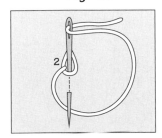

Fig. 11

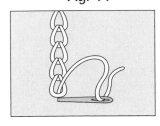

COUCHING STITCH

Referring to Fig. 12, lay the thread to be couched on the fabric; bring the needle up at 1 and go down at 2. Continue until entire thread length is couched.

Fig. 12

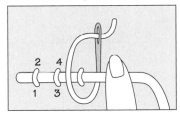

CROSS STITCH

Bring the needle up at 1 and go down at 2. Come up at 3 and go down at 4 (Fig. 13).

Fig. 13

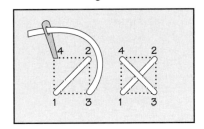

For the horizontal rows, work the stitches in 2 journeys (Fig. 14).

Fig. 14

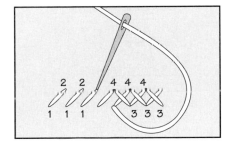

FERN STITCH

Referring to Fig. 15, work the central spine first then stitch a straight stitch either side of that spine. Bring needle up at 1, down at 2, up at 3, down at 4 and up at 5.

Fig. 15

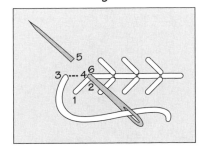

FLY STITCH

Refer to Fig. 16. Fly Stitch is also known as "Y" Stitch. It is worked making a V-shaped loop which is then tied down by a vertical Straight Stitch. Bring needle through the fabric out at the top and to the left of the line that is to be worked.

Fig. 16

FRENCH KNOT

Referring to Fig. 17, bring the needle up at 1. Wrap the floss once around the needle and insert the needle at 2, holding the floss end with non-stitching fingers. Tighten the knot; then, pull the needle through the fabric, holding the floss until it must be released. For larger knot, use more strands; wrap only once.

Fig. 17

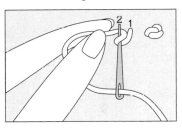

LAZY DAISY

Bring the needle up at 1; take the needle back down at 1 to form a loop and bring the needle up at 2. Keeping the loop below the point of the needle (Fig. 18), take the needle down at 3 to anchor the loop.

Fig. 18

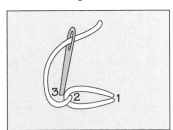

RUNNING STITCH

Referring to Fig. 19, make a series of straight stitches with the stitch length equal to the space between stitches.

Fig. 19

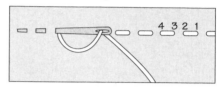

STEM STITCH

Referring to Fig. 20, come up at 1. Keeping the thread below the stitching line, go down at 2 and come up at 3. Go down at 4 and come up at 5.

Fig. 20

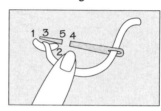

STRAIGHT STITCH

Referring to Fig. 21, come up at 1 and go down at 2.

Fig. 21

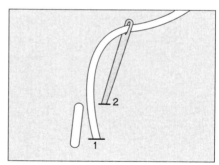

Needle Felting

Needle Felting uses wool roving. Wool roving can be purchased at fabric and crafts stores and online. It can be worked into shape by itself using a special needle felting needle and mat. Or, you can apply wool roving to a background fabric using a needle felting tool and mat. Lightly punch the needles to interlock the fibers and join the pieces without sewing or gluing. The brush-like mat allows the needles to easily pierce the fibers. We used the Clover® Felting Needle Tool to make our projects—it has a locking plastic shield that provides protection from the sharp needles.

Felting Sweaters

Felting sweaters brings the fibers in the sweater closer together to make it more compact. The texture becomes more interesting. Always use 100% wool sweaters when you wish to felt a sweater. Using sweaters with less than 90% wool will not work for felted sweater projects.

Place the sweater inside an old pillowcase and wash in very hot water in the washing machine. **Note:** Washing the sweater in the pillowcase keeps little fibers from getting into the machine works.

Use a little regular washing detergent when felting. Then rinse the sweaters in hot water and dry in a hot dryer. Press the wool before cutting out the pieces. Tightly felted wool does not ravel and can be left unfinished similar to using purchased wool felt.

Making Cones

1. Use a cone pattern such as the one on page 153 or make your own. Cut out the pattern and trace around it onto the paper you have chosen. Be sure to mark the dotted line and holes again on the printed paper. **Note:** If you can find paper that is printed with a pattern on both sides, then the inside and the outside of the cone will both look interesting. Cut out the cone. Punch the holes where the dots are on the pattern.

2. Carefully bend the paper around, curving the paper into a cone shape. See Fig. 22. Sometimes you might have to readjust the point to make it fit perfectly. Run a bead of glue along the edge of the cone and overlap to line it up with the dotted line.

3. Use a clothespin to hold the cone together while the glue dries. See Fig. 23.

4. Tie a knot in one end of the cord or ribbon. Starting from the outside of the cone, thread the ribbon or cording through one of the holes and then inside the other hole. Pull the knot tight up to the first side hole. See Fig. 24.

5. Adjust the length of the cording or ribbon to the length you want for the handle and tie a knot on the other side. See Fig. 25. Trim the ends of the ribbon. Add any other desired trims using crafts glue.

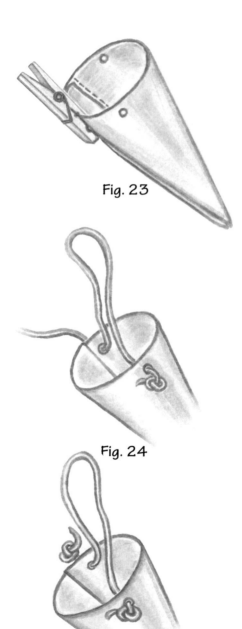

Fig. 22

Fig. 23

Fig. 24

Fig. 25

Patterns

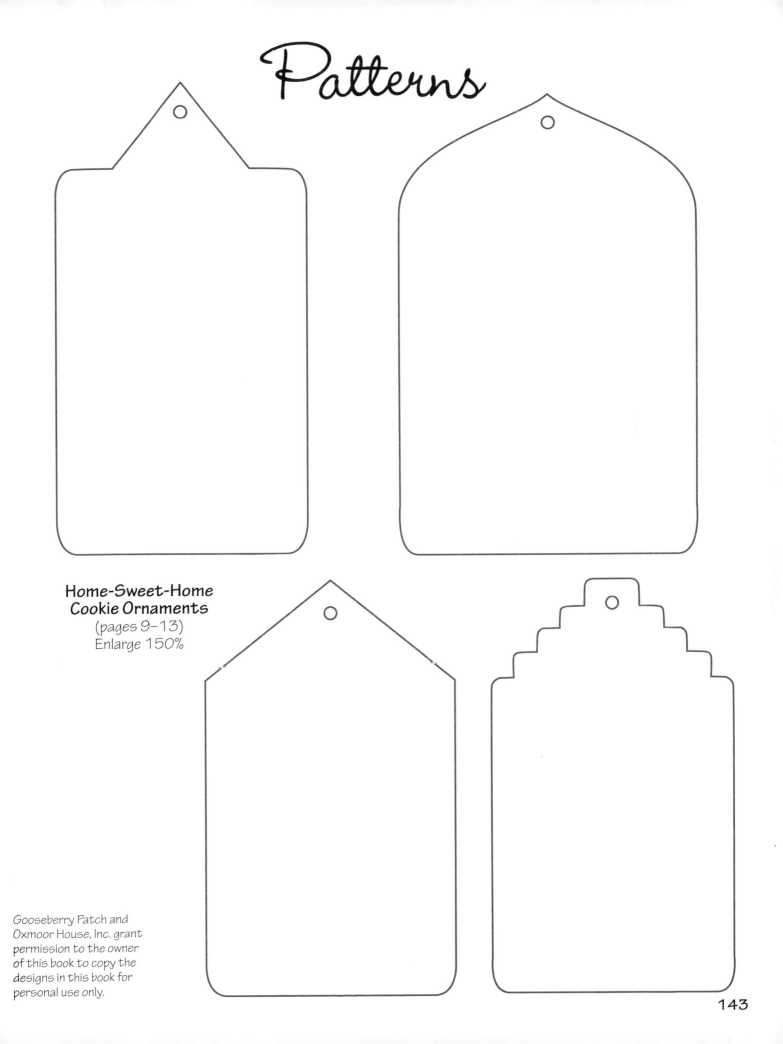

Home-Sweet-Home Cookie Ornaments
(pages 9-13)
Enlarge 150%

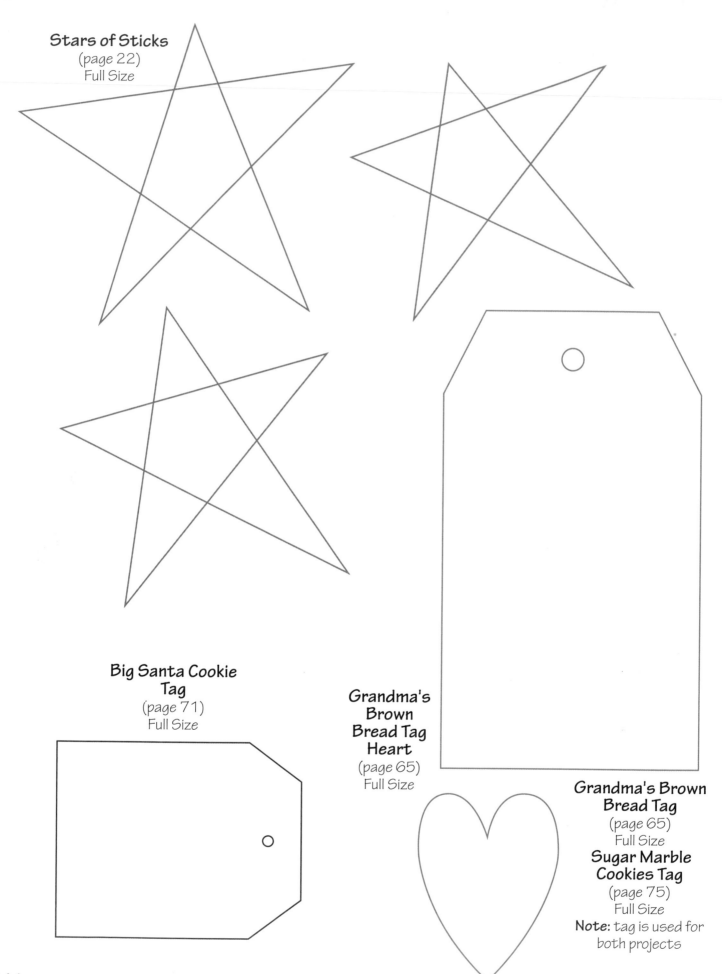

Stars of Sticks
(page 22)
Full Size

Big Santa Cookie Tag
(page 71)
Full Size

Grandma's Brown Bread Tag Heart
(page 65)
Full Size

Grandma's Brown Bread Tag
(page 65)
Full Size

Sugar Marble Cookies Tag
(page 75)
Full Size
Note: tag is used for both projects

**Tree Button
Card**
(page 41)
Full Size

**Gingerbread
Creamer Mix Tag**
(page 73)
Full Size

**Holiday Pretzel
Rods Tag**
(page 72)
Full Size

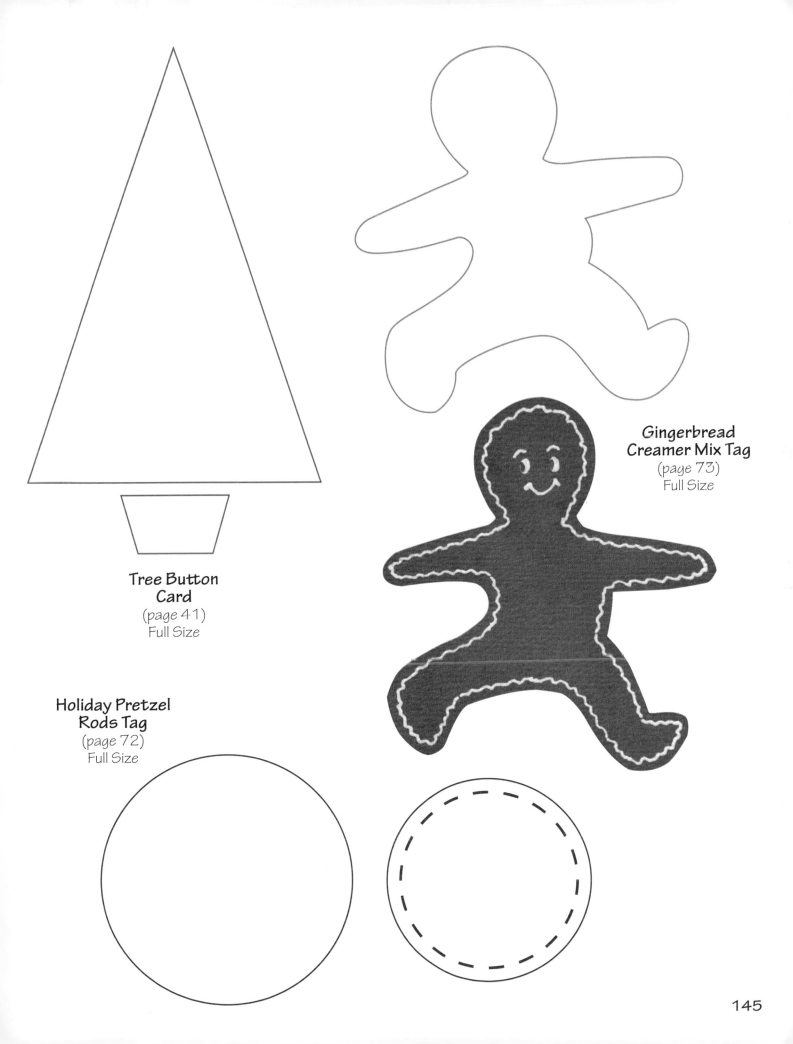

**Gingerbread Man
Ornaments**
(page 12)
Full Size

**Welcoming Apple
Basket**
(page 19)
Enlarge 200%

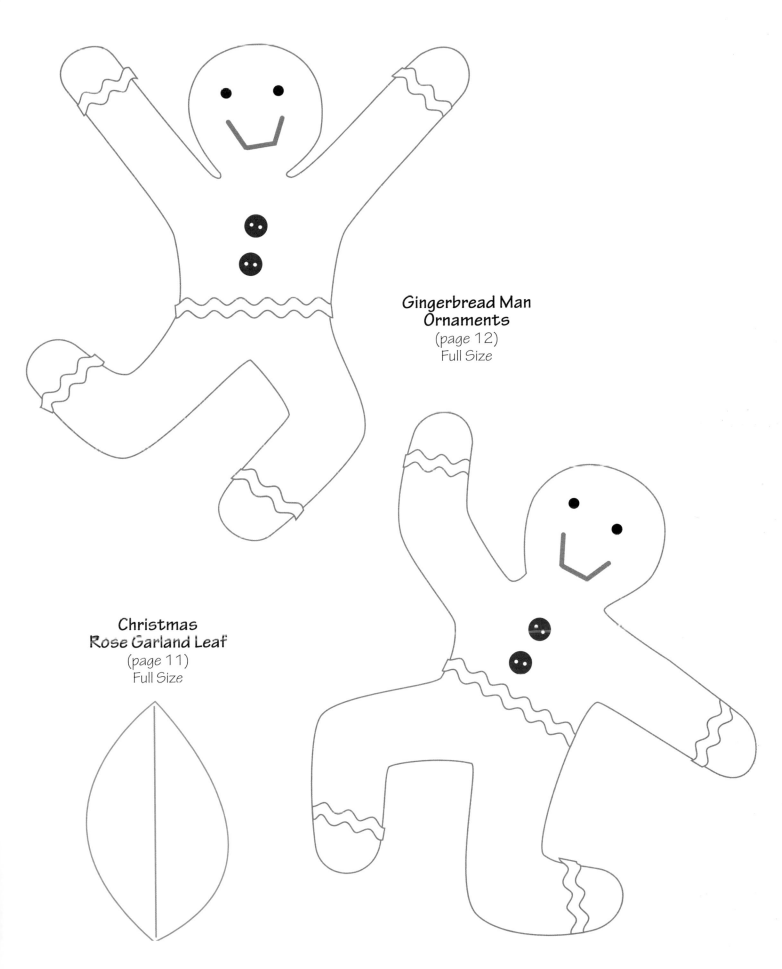

Gingerbread Man Ornaments
(page 12)
Full Size

Christmas Rose Garland Leaf
(page 11)
Full Size

Felt Mushroom Ornaments

(page 26)
Full Size

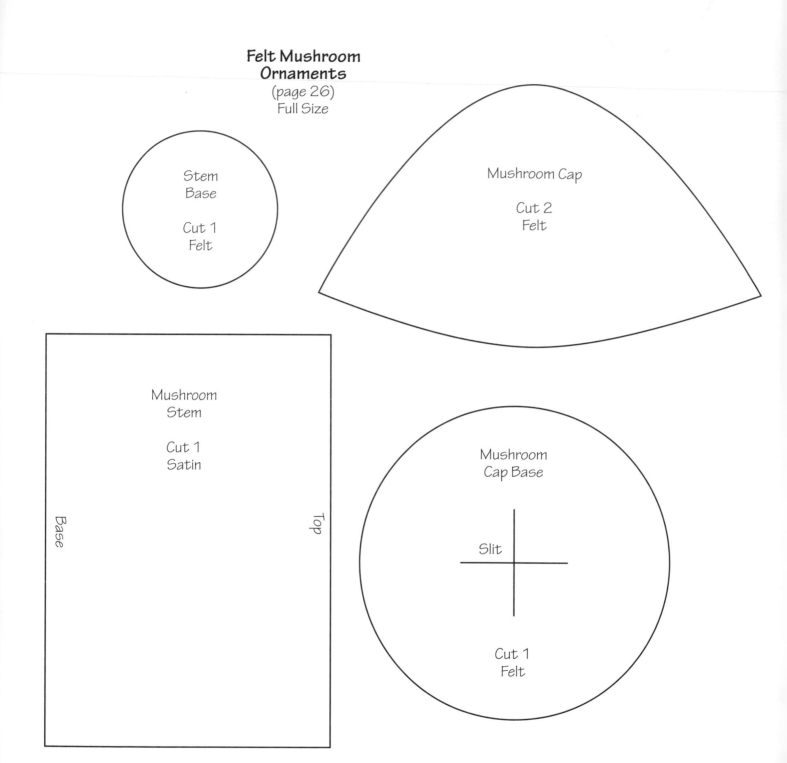

Stem
Base

Cut 1
Felt

Mushroom Cap

Cut 2
Felt

Mushroom
Stem

Cut 1
Satin

Base

Top

Mushroom
Cap Base

Slit

Cut 1
Felt

Friendly Owls
(page 39)
Full Size

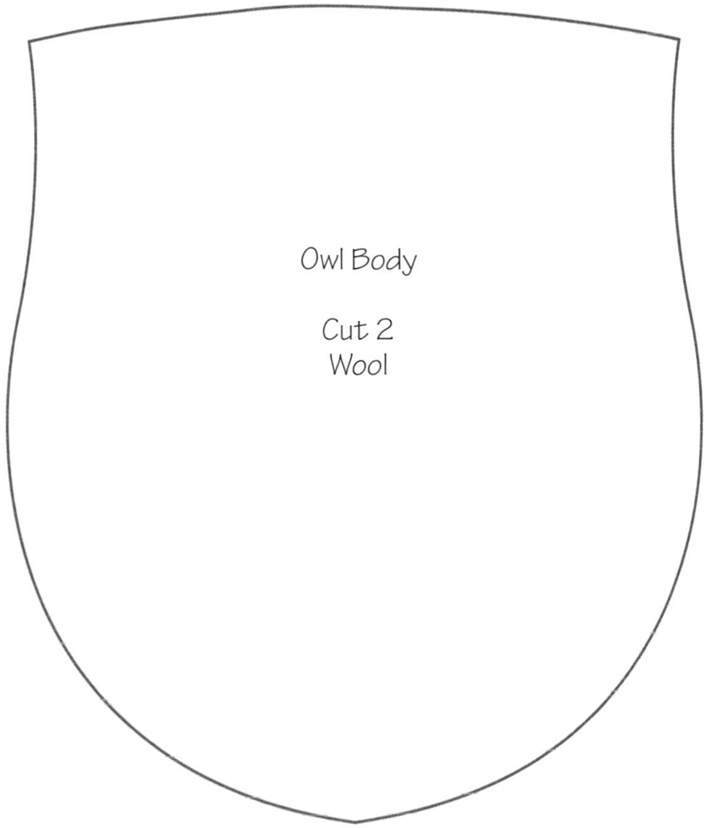

Owl Body

Cut 2
Wool

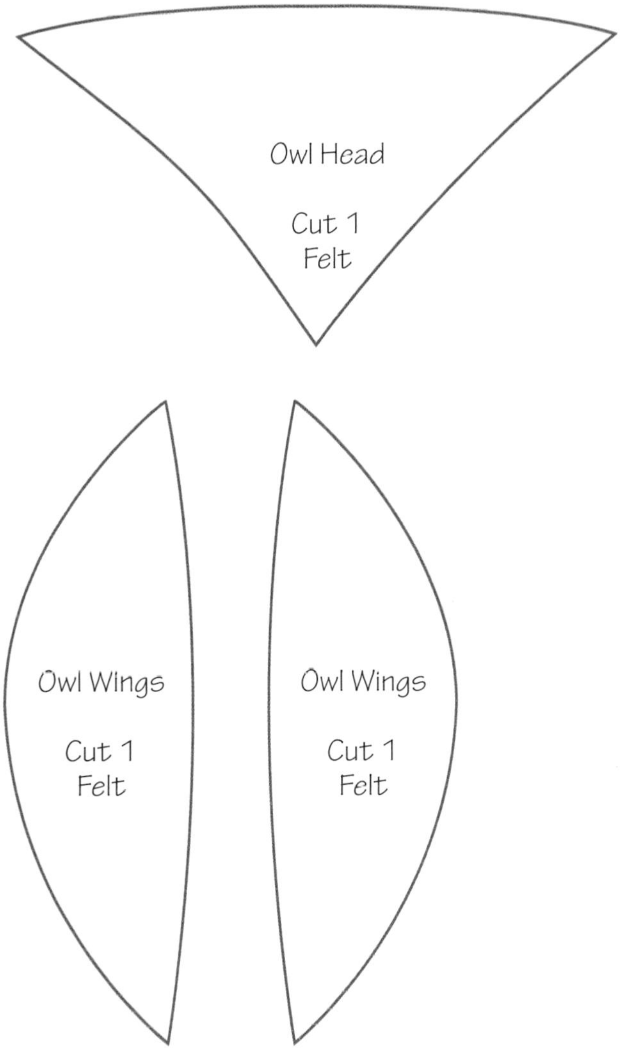

Owl Head

Cut 1
Felt

Owl Wings

Cut 1
Felt

Owl Wings

Cut 1
Felt

Colorful Circle Garland
(page 38)
Full Size

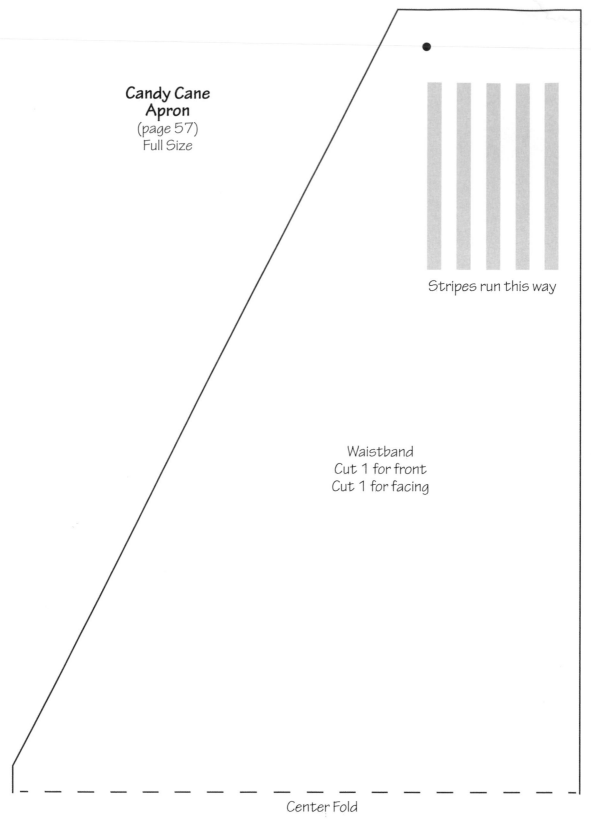

**Candy Cane
Apron**
(page 57)
Full Size

Stripes run this way

Waistband
Cut 1 for front
Cut 1 for facing

Top Waist

Center Fold

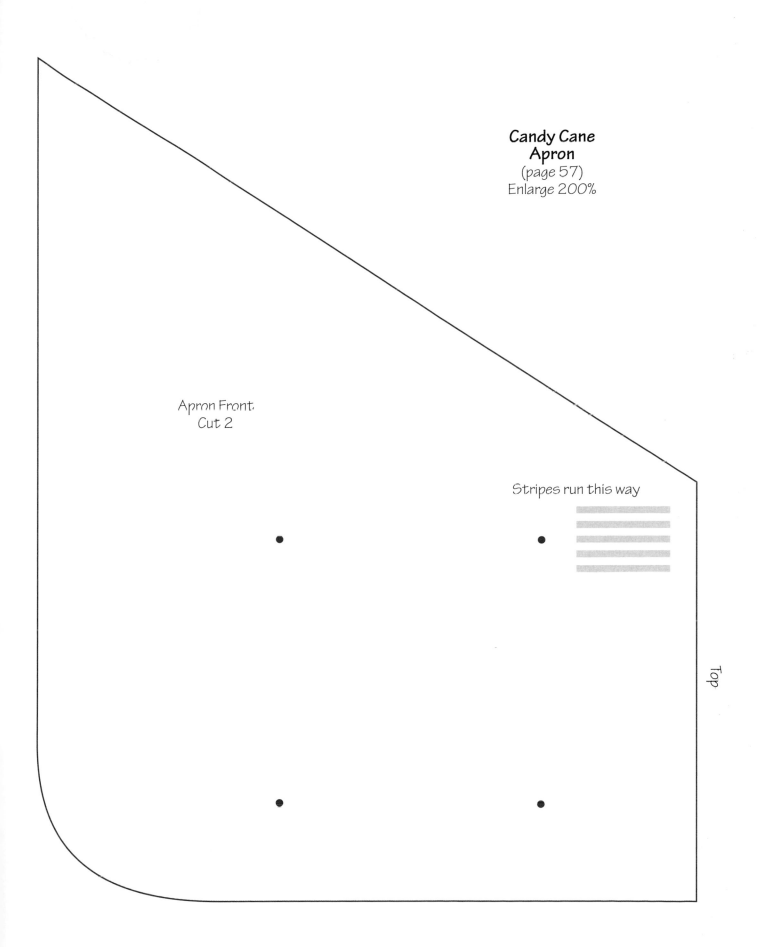

**Candy Cane
Apron**
(page 57)
Enlarge 200%

Apron Front.
Cut 2

Stripes run this way

Top

Quick Felt
Stocking
(page 60)
Enlarge 200%

Stocking Cuff

Cut 2

Sweet Chair
Back Slip
(page 52)
Enlarge 400%

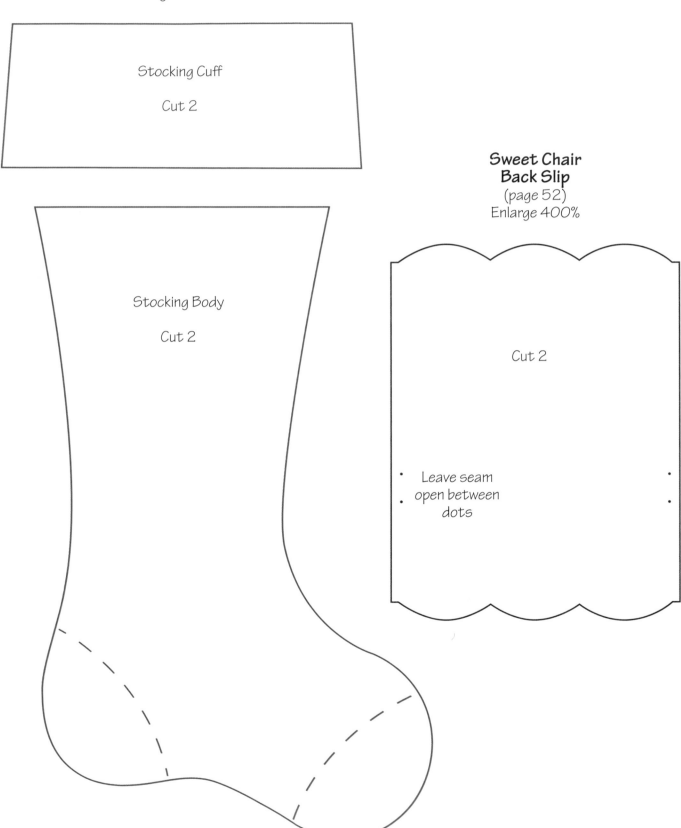

Stocking Body

Cut 2

Cut 2

· Leave seam
· open between
dots

·

·

Candy-Striped Cones
(page 56)
Full Size

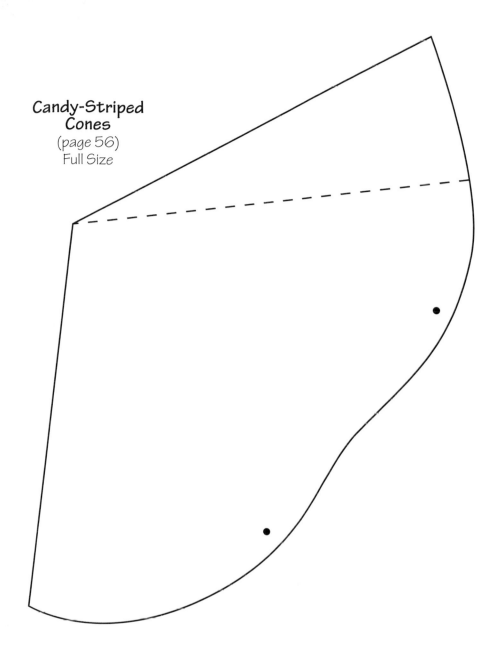

Needle-Felted Drink Cozies
(page 35)
Full Size

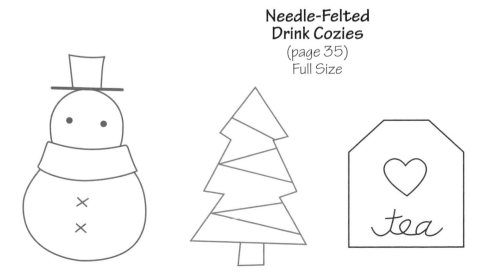

Vintage Christmas
Stocking Trio Stocking

(pages 14-15)

Enlarge 200%

Place Cuff Here
Stocking
Cut 2
Gingham, Calico or
Linen
Stocking Cuff
Cut 2
Gingham, Calico or
LInen
Stocking Toe
Cut 2
Gingham, Calico or
LInen

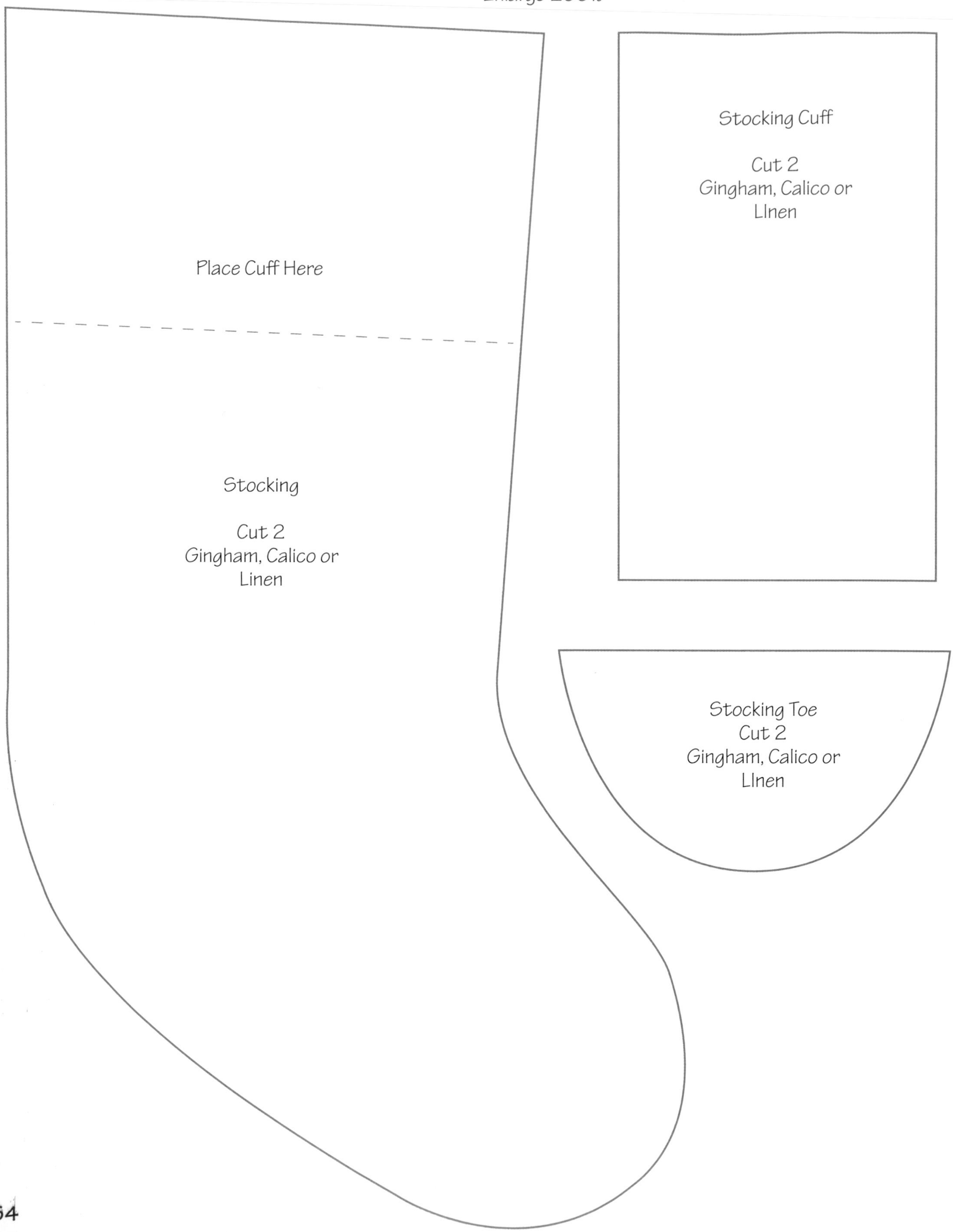

Vintage Christmas Stocking Trio
Liner
(pages 14-15)
Enlarge 200%

Stocking Liner

Cut 2
Lining Fabric

Leave seam
open between
dots

Kaleidoscope Magnets
(page 30)
Size to fit

Gingham Rickrack Apron
(page 18)

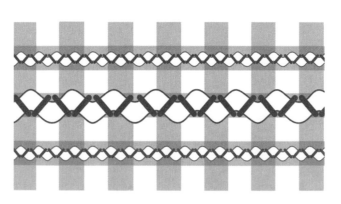

Mini Rickrack

Medium Rickrack

Mini Rickrack

Christmas-Red Cross-Stitch Apron
(page 19)

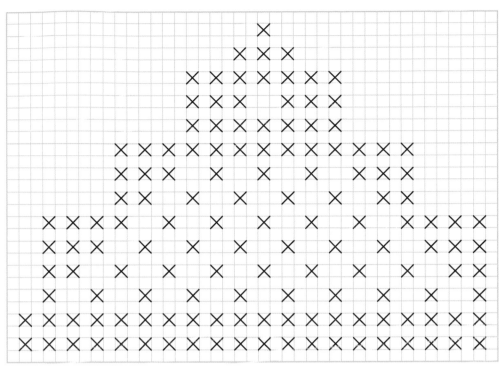

Apron Front Bottom
Trim

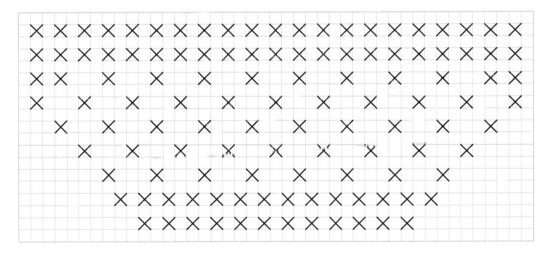

Pocket Trim

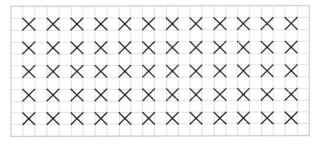

Apron String Trim

Note: Measurements noted assume working cross-stitches from bottom to top.

Project Index

Recipe Index

Credits

We want to extend a warm "thank you!" to so many people who helped to create this book:

We want to thank Jay Wilde Photography and Dean Tanner at Primary Image for sharing their excellent photographic skills with us. We also want to thank Jennifer Peterson for sharing her beautiful cookie decorating talents with us!

It takes quality supplies to make beautiful projects. These are some of the companies that we used to make the crafts and decorating projects in the book: DMC Corporation for embroidery floss, Clover Needlecraft, Inc., for needle felting supplies, Bazzill Basics for many of the paper crafts, National Nonwovens for superior felting supplies, Bobs Candies for candy sticks and canes and Caron Simply Soft® for yarns.

Thank you to Martin Schmidt & Sons in Portland, Oregon for the beautiful Christmas trees, fresh greenery and wreaths we used in the photos.

A special thank you to Donna Chestnut for sharing her vintage clock collection with us. We would like to thank Eunella Neymeyer for letting us use her vintage toys. We would also like to thank Ardith Field for sharing her antique linens and vintage kitchen collection with us.

We want to thank our special models: Michelle, Elizabeth and Jan for sharing their modeling talents with us.

A very special thank you to Sharon and Craig Northouse, who allowed us to photograph some of the projects in their beautiful home.

If these cozy Christmas ideas have inspired you to look for more Gooseberry Patch® publications, find us online at www.gooseberrypatch.com and see what's new. We're on Facebook and Twitter too, so you can keep up with us even more often!